Within the Arm's Reach:

Personal Protection for a

New Millennium

By Clifford W. Stewart

Within the Arm's Reach: Personal Protection for a New Millennium

By Clifford W. Stewart

Copyright © 2025 I&I SPORTS SUPPLY. All rights reserved.
Published by I&I SPORTS SUPPLY
ISBN 978-0-934489-39-3

Table of Contents

4 Foreword
6 Acknowledgements
10 Introduction
15 What Is Within Arm's Reach?
16 Executive Protection/Anti-Terrorism
24 Testimonials
27 The Protectors
34 The Foundation
37 Awareness — "The Casino"
40 Awareness — The The Super Principle
41 Personal Awareness
42 Awareness Destruction
43 Openings
45 "Dining with Mr. T."
48 The Ninja in the Overcoat
51 The Three Stages of Conflict
52 The Westwood Assault
56 Post-Assault
57 Hand-to-Hand and Beyond
59 The Student Types
60 Methods of Instruction
61 The Formula of W.A.R.
62 P.O.W of W.A.R.
66 Limb Associated Points (L.A.P.)
80 Hostage Retrieval
82 P.A.L.'s 14-Count (Level One)
98 Protective Assault Control (P.A.C.)
112 The Edge of W.A.R.
113 The Impact of W.A.R.
114 The W.A.R Chest
115 Tools of the Trade
123 Definitions

Foreword

By Master Instructor Massad Ayoob

Early in this book, its author invites you to ask, "Who the hell is Cliff Stewart?" It's a question I don't have to ask. I've known Cliff for more than 15 years — as student and instructor, as friend and peer.

The guy has more black belts than a men's store, and in many of the disciplines he has studied he is a master instructor — that is, a trainer of other trainers.

When you're rich and famous, you need two kinds of CPAs. One is the Certified Public Accountant who will help you keep as much as possible of the money you've earned; the other is a Close Protection Agent like Cliff, to keep you alive to enjoy it.

Cliff Stewart knows his stuff. I've worked with many of his contemporaries who studied under masters such as Dan Inosanto at the same time Cliff was there. The martial arts world can be a jealous place, with more than its share of prima donnas. Yet, from Graciela Casillas to Paul Vunak, each of Cliff's contemporaries I've spoken with gives Stewart the highest praise. It's a rare man who can be that well-liked and that highly respected at the same time in such an ego-charged environment. It says a lot for the grace and professionalism of Casillas and Vunak, of course, but it says even more about Cliff Stewart.

Cliff and I are a two-way street. I was gratified to learn that Cliff could instantly put into real-world practice everything I showed him.

But he didn't just take; he also gave back. One day during a teaching break on the grounds of the Long Beach Police Academy range, my colleague, Mike Izumi, and I were showing Cliff a handgun retention technique we had learned from a master instructor elsewhere. Cliff said softly, "Consider this," and showed us a much simpler movement from pentjak silat that more easily defeated the same attack. Mike and I worked with that technique for hours, determined that indeed it was better, and we incorporated it into the bag of defensive tricks we taught our students at Lethal Force Institute. Thousands of our graduates have learned to protect themselves and their guns with the "belly-wipe" technique and they have Cliff Stewart to thank for it.

The Stewart legend lives not just in the dojo of Los Angeles, but in its streets as well. A few years ago Cliff was out in the wee hours picking up some necessities for his newborn child, and was set upon by three street muggers who suffered what I've come to call "a sudden and acute failure of the victim selection process." One swung at Cliff with an iron pipe. The fight was on.. .and it was over in seconds. When police got there, they found three men on the ground, all either unconscious or in too much pain to move or speak. All had suffered either major broken bones or serious internal injuries... and, significantly, none was outwardly marked or had shed a drop of blood.

The only one bleeding was Stewart, slightly injured by a glancing blow of the pipe he had deflected from its original skull-crushing path before he began returning force. It took the officers a while to figure out that "the last man standing" was the intended victim, not the perpetrator. But, once that was sorted out, no one appreciated the justice of the outcome more than the responding officers...

I've seen the gentle side of Cliff Stewart. When watching him with the woman he loves or delicately cradling his baby son, you see a very large teddy bear. But watch him in the training environment or in the field and you realize the bear is really a grizzly in disguise. Cliff keeps the grizzly behind a very strong barred door, but it's always right at the door, a fraction of a second away from a conscious decision to release it when nothing less powerful can protect the innocent.

There is a lesson in this, and it's a lesson that Cliff Stewart emphasizes in his Within Arm's Reach training program. It's a lesson this good man teaches by example. The lesson is: the bear doesn't control Cliff; Cliff controls the bear. He teaches his students that just because there are wolves out there doesn't mean you have to become a wolf yourself. It will suffice to be the sheepdog.

Cliff Stewart possesses an awesome degree of knowledge and destructive power. The point he drives into his W.A.R. students is that possessing power doesn't mean you have to use it. Often, he makes clear, the greatest expression of that power is to dominate a threatening situation to where you don't need to unleash it. Avoidance, he points out, is the ultimate victory.

It's one thing to hear that from a wimp you know couldn't bear to face conflict. It becomes more credible when you hear it from a man who is a veteran of conflict and has left a long trail of strong, violent men prostrate and unconscious behind him. Such a man is Cliff Stewart.

I manage crisis and teach crisis management for a living. I know the difference between the professionals and the phonies. Cliff Stewart is a professional. When he talks, I listen. So do other professionals.

And so should you. **Massad Ayoob**

The author of numerous textbooks on defensive use of force, Massad Ayoob is the founder of Lethal Force Institute. Cross-trained to master instructor level with unarmed police defensive tactics, firearms, batons, and weapon retention and disarming, Ayoob has been a police officer for more than 26 years and since 1987 has been chair of the Firearms and Deadly Force Committee of the American Society of Law Enforcement Trainers, where he also served for several years on the Ethics Committee. A former national, regional, and state champion in combat shooting, Ayoob was named the Outstanding American Handgunner of

Acknowledgements

The paths I have chosen have always been the roads less traveled. I have always had a strong desire to be the best and learn from the very best. Hand-to-hand combat continues to be one of my fascinations, along with every type of martial art. I would like to thank those who helped, taught, instructed, corrected, shared, supported, exchanged, encouraged, listened, were thrown, struck, locked and knocked out to help with my personal growth, survival and the development of *Within Arms Reach*.

I have learned from the best Master Instructors in the martial sciences in the fields of Defensive Tactics, Use of Lethal Force, Edged Weapons, Close-Quarter Firearms, Advance Police Survival and Tactics, VIP Protection, Explosive Entry, and Special Weapons.

I've studied and practiced in historic settings with great instructors, world champions, and masters and grandmasters, including:

- Judo at Senna dojo;
- Shotokan with master Nakamura, who taught me discipline, as well as the value of hard and powerful kicks and punches;
- Hapkido with grandmasters Sea Oh Choi and Bong Soo Han, who taught me the true high art of self-defense.

Special thanks go to:
- Grandmaster Steve Muhammad of the BKF style of kenpo, who shared his knowledge of hand-speed development and application. I call him my brother.

Grandmaster Steve Muhammad

- Grandmaster Jerry Smith, my brother in arms and life, who taught me how to express evil intent in my self-defense techniques as well as a winning attitude.
- Grandmaster Ed Parker, a true genius, who was kind enough to share — without restrictions — his knowledge of kenpo and security.
- Master Instructor and Lethal Force Expert Massad Ayoob, for his real-world teaching of the justifiable use of force and how to survive its aftermath and the basic tactics and skills needed to control an armed assault.
- Grandmaster Dr. Maung Gyi of Bando America, for his interest in my Within Arm's Reach method, suggestions and silent manner of teaching.
- Grandmaster Taika Seiyu Oyata and his instructors, for allowing me a glimpse at their life protection art.
- Paul Dalton, who gave me my first full-contact session and taste of jeet kune do. He called his system chuan fa.
- Professor Ron Chapel, who is the world's leading authority on kenpo concepts and application. He shared with me the deepest levels of kenpo; and his friend, grandmaster Joe Lewis, considered by *Black Belt* magazine to

Grandmaster Wally Jay

Guro Larry Hartsell

be the greatest heavyweight kickboxer of all time. Also one of the greatest martial scientists of all time, Lewis taught me about the principles of combat and how to use them; about pain and how to take it; and the psychological aspect of fighting.

• Master Instructor and funny guy, Dave Smith, who taught me the psychology of survival and advanced police tactics.

• Grandmaster Wally Jay, for teaching me his small circle concepts for applying energy and pain into locks and knockouts.

• To guro Ted Lucay Lucay, for his sharing and caring. We miss you.

• Grandmaster guro Dan Inosanto, who taught me how to blend all my systems into one and started my understanding of the blade and stick.

• Sifu Jerry Poteet, for his great trapping skills and for teaching me how to trap, when to trap and why to trap.

• Master Firearms Instructor Bruce Thompson, Small Arms Manage-ment (SAM) and my assistant Archangel, who has been my buddy and back-up for over a decade. He's one tough son of a gun.

• Master jeet kune do grappler and guro Larry Hartsell, who shared his friendship, expertise and energy. I call him my brother.

- Master Chai Sirisute, for your instruction and street combat insights of muay Thai.
- Brother Ahati Kilindi Iyi, who taught me the ancient way of the dance for fighting with the hands, body and weapons.
- Master Defense Tactics Instructor and Survival System Designer Bruce Siddle PPCT, for starting me on my journey of learning tactical use of pressure point attacks.
- Master Hideki Frazier, for his unselfish giving of his knowledge and time.
- Grandmaster George Dillman, for sharing his wealth of information and expertise.
- Grandmaster Rick Moneymaker, for his kindness and selflessness in answering the many questions I had regarding the uses of pressure points.
- The Iron guro, Vince Gironda, for sharing how to train. You were a man way ahead of your time and we miss you.
- Grandmaster Angel Cabales, for his unselfish teaching of the art of serrada eskrima and its real-world survival usage.
- Master Instructor Dennis Kennedy, for his unique firearms training program and expertise in understanding concealed weapons requirements nationwide. You are my brother in personal protection and life.
- To grandmaster Sultan, who continues to amaze me with his great skill, kindness and giving.
- Master Dennis Newsome, truly a warrior's warrior, master guro and friend.
- Master Graciela Casillas, who helped develop the Within Arm's Reach method. She shared and exchanged combative concepts, edged weapons

Grandmaster Angel Cabales

usage, boxing, and straight stick combat street applications. I am proud to call her one of my dearest friends.
- Ben Rosen, Green Beret Special Operation Tactics and Firearm Expert, who taught me Advanced Tactics and Firearm Skills for anti-terrorism, special weapons and operations.
- Pendekar Paul deThouars, my mentor, teacher and adviser. He has taught me how to destroy attackers through the deadly arts of serak and bukti negara pukulan penjat silat by understanding the structure, nerve sites, balance points, and internal and external disruptions of the human body. He is a man among men, a warrior's king, a professor's professor of the martial sciences, a man of truth, conviction, ethics, warmth, commitment and fairness. He is like a father to me. I love, respect and thank him for his patience, time, knowledge and suggestions.

Cliff with Pendekar Paul deThouars and Bando Grandmaster Or. Maung Gyi.

* Mr. and Mrs. Adham and family, for their royal support and encouragement in the writing of this book. Also, for allowing me to experience the world and its many cultures, peoples and venues. I thank them for permitting me to see places most people only dream about. They have encouraged my teaching of Within Arm's Reach seminars worldwide and made sure when possible I was available to accept a number of personal awards — sometimes at their expense. He and his beautiful wife have always given me their support far above and beyond the responsibility an employer has for his employee. I wish to thank them because without their consideration, support and caring this book wouldn't be possible.

• My IMF force: Taroo, Bruce, Phil Robb, Shaka, Cooper, Miller, William Nealy, Robert Moore, Jerry Smith, Larry Hartsell, John Arthur and Robert D., Greg Wilkinson, Dr. Berry, Rick the Cobra, Gino, Carlton James, Gene Clark, Alain Migeotte Lambert, Rick Tarin, Don Shabazz, and Darryl Carson.

• My students and instructors, for all their help.

• My first black-belt class grads "OG's": Prof. Mike Belzer, Karen Dean, Bill Haas, Don Shabazz, David and Sandra Feldman, Mike Frescas, Paul Mirader, Jeff Chean, Wynn Armstrong, Breck Cooney, Lawrence Boydston, Mark Wall, Witney West, Lisa Bruder, Don Havey, Keith Thomas, and Stud Ilium. They were granted their black belts by a board of master black belts from different methods and styles. Also a number of my non-pro/martial artist instructors were already accomplished black belts in their own styles and I thank them for their faith in my Within Arm's Reach program.

• Professional Basic Instructors Lt. Kathy Zyach N.Y.U., Captain Dennis Webb, Lt. Sonny Alicie, David Robinson — Prince Instructors for tactic teams for Prince Williams — Manassas ADC.

• To the other toughest two-man team I ever met — Lt. Allen Barr and Ofc. Daryl Vega, CFW Regional Jail Tactic Team;

• Editor Karen Dean, whose help, sacrifice and energy helped me write this book. And Editor Dave Cater, whose faith and encouragement helped me bring this to print.

And to everyone I may have left out. No man is an island; I thank you all from the bottom of my heart.

Cliff Stewart 3rd-degree or higher

Introduction

I have been in the martial arts sciences for over 40 years. I have studied various forms of combat and have attained advanced-level black belts and/or instructor levels in numerous methods of martial sciences.

Working exclusively in the executive protection field for over 25 years, I have provided personal protection services for a number of high-profile clients in such varied locales as France, Spain, England, Africa, Canada, Central America, Italy, the Middle East, Australia, North Africa, Hong Kong, South America, and the United States. Spending so many years guarding celebrities has earned me the nickname "Bodyguard to the Stars."

Those pursuing a career as a Close Protection Agent (CPA) will find it both difficult and exciting, boring and exhilarating. It is a multifaceted, dangerous and challenging job. One minute you may be arranging a dinner reservation at a posh Beverly Hills, Calif, restaurant. The next minute you may be flying off to Paris, patrolling on a yacht on the Mediterranean or guarding a murder witness at a federal courthouse. The CPA must understand his first responsibility is the protection of human life.

I designed the *Within Arms Reach* (W.A.R.) method to teach personal protection to elite teams (also known as CPAs) worldwide. W.A.R. is composed of a number of components, including hand-to-hand combat firearms, impact and edged weapons, hostage retrieval, and protection skills. W.A.R. also relates directly to mental, personal and psychological management of combat. The emphasis here is on fear management, ego control, instinct control and awareness.

This book marks the first time I share *Within Arm's Reach* with the public. You will learn through my real-world experiences — not a classroom, gym or martial

James Garner

At Wolfgang Puck's Spago Restaurant in Beverly Hills, Calif. (right).

Private Jets....

Limos....

Paris in the springtime or by sea – anytime!

arts studio — how these elements are incorporated.

This book also will give you:

- The skills needed to become a Personal Protection Elite Professional or CPA;
- The CPA standards of personal development that will set you apart from the wanna-bes ;
- The "Father" principle of all protection principles;
- The physical, tactical, audio and emotional elements of awareness;
- Positioning to maximize your protective circle;
- The Three-Way Partnership and how CPAs use them;
- The different types of protectors from the military, federal, state, police and private sectors;
- Why a law enforcement background is not necessarily good for executive protection;
- Which principle in executive protection always comes first;
- The physical principles needed to control any close-quarter attack; and
- The keys to improving any personal defense system and the concepts and principles that will help you protect others.

Also covered will be why martial arts is not the answer for personal protection; how to escalate any technique without changing it; and why other experts are in the same position as martial artists.

You'll be taught the physical intervention skills required for the personal protection profession and why you need more skills in the private sector than any other. Also revealed will be the different stages of assaults and what you need to know about them to keep your client alive and yourself out of jail. Without this understanding you can never become a true CPA.

Within Arms Reach will teach you the "tricks of the trade", including: the best way to open a car door for a client; how to prevent unwanted pictures from being taken without risking an arrest; two ways of protective scanning to cover 360 degrees in one position; the do's and don'ts of the trade; and the deadly sins that will get you fired every time.

Muhammad Ali

What is Within Arm's Reach?

A lot of you are probably wondering, "Who in the hell is Cliff Stewart and why should I pay good money to learn from him?" I don't blame you for asking that question. Let me tell you who I am and why you'll get your money's worth from this book.

My background is both extensive and diverse. I am an expert in the areas of Personal Protection/Management/Supervision, Anti-Terrorism, Firearms Training, Defensive Tactics, and Martial Sciences.

I have worked for the past 20 years as the Director of Corporate Security for a Royal Middle Eastern family. Also during the last quarter-century I have held comparable positions and duties, which included providing personal protection, conducting investigations, and managing and training large staffs of security personnel — undercover and plain-clothed, armed and unarmed.

I have also provided protection for various attorneys, corporate executives and their families, members of royal families and foreign diplomats, and a number of celebrities, including: Motown recording artists Stevie Wonder, Smokey Robinson, and the Four Tops; former heavyweight champion Muhammad Ali; *Hustler* magazine publisher Larry Flynt; actress Joan Collins; and even Mr. T, star of the "A-Team" television series. While working as Director of Corporate Security for Larry Flynt Enterprises, I was responsible for the personal security of Mr. and Mrs. Larry Flynt and their family, and oversaw the training and managing of both the security and personal protection teams.

The "A-Team"

From 1975-1979, I provided management services that included supervision of 100-to-200 security and support personnel for stadium concerts accommodating in excess of 40,000 fans.

My career has consisted extensively of management, consulting and supervisory positions. I also have prepared a number of personal protection and security budgets totaling in excess of $ 1 million annually.

Executive Protection/Anti-Terrorism

My training has been varied and extensive because that is what is required of an elite Professional. My Professional training includes having completed the Aegis Executive Protection Course; the Argenbright International Training Institute (Advance Executive Protection and Executive Protection); the Cobray Protection Training Camp; Ordinance Exposition Executive Protection; and International Terrorism/Anti-Terrorism. I also trained with my good friend, United States Army Green Beret, Lt. Col. Ben Rosen, Retired, who was in charge of Special Operations, Counterterrorism, Firearms and Tactics.

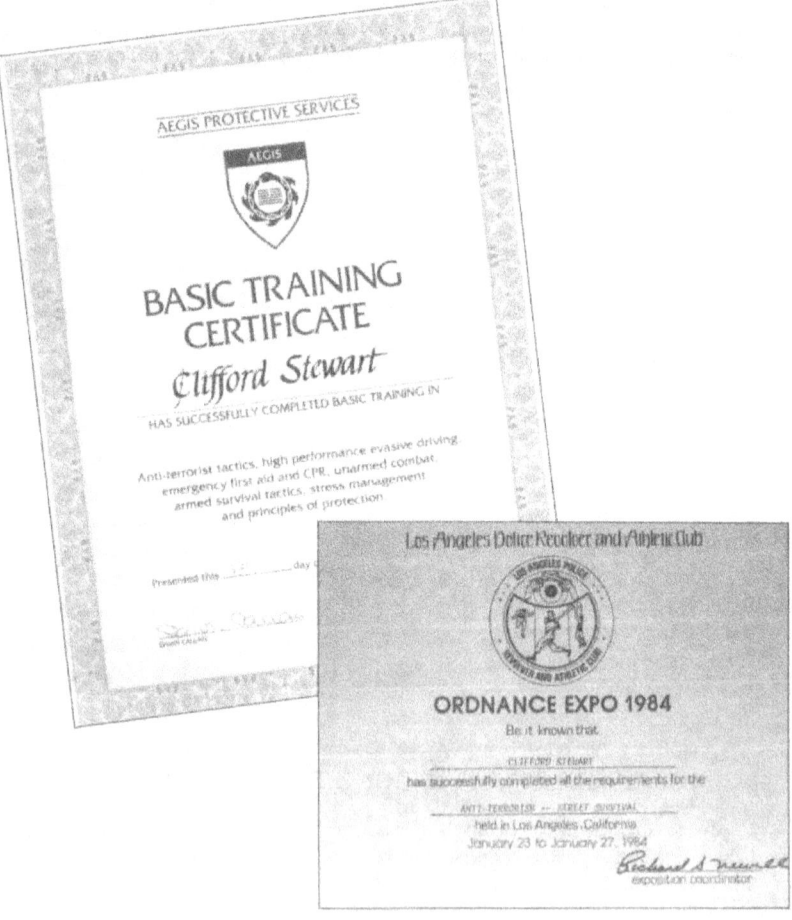

Firearms Training

As a Professional, firearms training is a must. To that end, I completed various courses in firearms training. They include: Bruce Thompsons Small Arms Management, which featured basic, intermediate and advanced courses in handguns and shotguns; Special Weapons Training and Advanced S.W.A.T. Weapons and Tactics at Rio Hondo College; Executive Protection Firearms, which involved Intermediate Executive Protection, Advanced Executive Protection, Close Quarter Battle, Advanced Close Quarter Battle; and Close Quarter Battle Instructors Course with Master Instructor Dennis Kennedy. The I.P.S Executive Protection Hand Gun course consisted of Special Weapons & Tactics and Explosive Entry. I also completed the series of National Rifle Association Instructor Courses, specifically training in Personal Protection, Home Protection and Pistol. At the Lethal Force Institute, I completed LFI-1 and LFI-2 taught by Master Instructor Massad Ayoob.

I am a Master Instructor in a number of Defensive Tactics systems, among them: A.P.S. Close Quarter Combat; Defensive Edge System; Pressure Point Control Tactics; Knife Counter Knife, Chapel's Arrest and Control Tactics; and I.P.S. Close Quarter Combat. I have been an instructor in PR-24, Straight Baton/PR-24 and Straight Arm Baton Tactics. I have been a consultant and an instructor for the Aegis Executive Protection. I am a Master Guro and Board Member in the Indonesian art known as
pentjak silat (bukti negara) and a practitioner of serak.

I hold the rank of basic instructor/black belt and/or professor level in the following martial art disciplines: ahati, 5 level method; hapkido; Jun Fan/jeet kune do; judo; jiu-jitsu; Dillman's Pressure Point Attack; kali/serrada/eskrima; kenpo; Lewis Method of Karate; muay Thai boxing; and shotokan. I am the Founder, Director and Senior Instructor of Within Arm's Reach (W.A.R.), which was designed for Executive Protection Specialists and other elite professional teams/units.

Survival and Tactics

I have completed the Caliber Press Street Survival for Law Enforcement series, which consists of Street Survival, Tactical Edge, Advanced Officer Street Survival, and W.I.N. Additionally, I completed I.P.S. Special Operations and Tactics and finished both the PPCT Advanced Police Survival and Advanced Officer Survival classes. Other training includes, Advanced Medical Red Cross and CPR; Bondurant Anti-Terrorist Corporate Course; I.P.S. Counter Ambush Driving course; and Randall Stunt Driving School. I also instruct psychomotor skills.

Certifications

I have received certification in Scuba Diving, Stress Management, Violent Conflict/Multiple Opponent Confrontation, Teaching the Trainer, and Weapons Awareness.

I hold teaching credentials and/or certifications in Advanced Security and VIP Executive Protection; California Post Secondary Teaching; and own Carry Concealed Weapon permits for California, Florida, Idaho and other states.

I am also a certified Defensive Tactics Instructor, Edged Weapons Instructor, Expert Witness Testimony/Precedent Setting Security Training, and N.R.A. Firearms Instructor.

Cliff instructing the Maryland S.W.A.T. team.

Teaching Experience

I have engaged in coundess seminars, college courses, been a guest lecturer, and have taught Within Arm's Reach to numerous S.W.A.T. and military units. More specifically, 1 have taught a number of 250-hour VIP Protection courses, and numerous two- and three-day courses, which have resulted in thousands of graduates.

While an instructor at St. Mary's College in Maryland, I developed, taught and demonstrated a course called The History and Applications of the Martial Arts in the United States to one of the largest classes on campus. I have been a guest lecturer for Master Instructor Massad Ayoob at the Lethal Force Institute. Additionally, I was the first person to take Lethal Force 1 and 2 back-to-back with over 80 demanding hours of instruction. Recently, I taught a two-day Within Arm's Reach seminar to the Montgomery County Police Tactical Section and a number of other S.W.A.T. teams.

THE AMERICAN TEACHERS ASSOCIATION OF THE MARTIAL ARTS

Whereas This Instructor Has Demonstrated Outstanding Teaching Ability, Mastery of the Knowledge and Skills of the Martial Arts, and Understanding of the Philosophical Truths

The Ranking Committee of the ATAMA Certifies That _Clifford Stewart_ Is Hereby Awarded the Masters Teaching Rank _Professor 8th Degree_ In the Martial Art of _Within - Arms Reach_

Professional Affiliations

I am a Defensive Tactics Consultant for the Los Angeles Police Department and for a number of adult correctional facilities in Virginia, including Manassas, Virginia Correctional Facility, Montgomery County S.W.A.T. Teams, and S.W.A.T. teams in DeKalb County. I have consulted for the Department of the United States Army and Navy Special Operations SEALs Team One. I am also an Impact Protection Consultant.

Professional Honors

The City of Los Angeles and Mayors Tom Bradley and Richard Riordan recognized and awarded me the title of grandmaster. Also, I was presented with an award for gang diversion work done in Youth Services, which was presented by the City of Los Angeles. I have been inducted into the Martial Arts Hall of Fame. In September, 1999, I was honored by being inducted into the World Head of Family Sokeship Council, International Hall of Fame as a Master of Self-Defense. This organization is the world's most prestigious Grandmaster's Council. I was honored by the American Bando Association and Dr. Mating Gyi, Chief Instructor, as an honoree at its 2000 National Middle-Style Tournament, where I also was named an honorary member. I am a member of Who's Who of the International and American Teachers of the Martial Arts and an International Board Member.

Publications

I have been interviewed for and appeared in numerous magazines, among them: *Black Belt magazine*, "Pre-Assault Assessment," June, 1989; *Black Belt magazine*, "Assault Assessment," July, 1989; *Jeet Kune Do Grappling*, Volume 2, Hartsell and Tackett; *Masters of Kung-Fu*, "It's aW.A.R. Out There!" September, 1993; *Inside Karate:* "Black Belt Bodyguards".

Books include: *The Complete Book of Handguns* by Massad Ayoob. The article was entitled, "Contact Distance Gun Defense Tactics", 1999; *Hollywood Babylon* "P.I. to the Stars" by Don Crutchfield. (I appear in two chapters, one involving Griffin O'Neal (Ryan O'Neal's son) and the other involving Roseanne Barr's wedding); "Not an Easy Target," by Paxton Quigley, 1994; "How to be a Black Belt in the Art of Life," by Jack and Beverly Gustafson; *American Survival Guide,* November, 1997, "Close Quarter Defensive Training From Within Arm's Reach (W.A.R.)" by Paul Hantke; "Personal Security" by Dave Cater, June, 1998; *Karate International,* "JKD the Next Generation," by Jerry Beasley, E.D.D. 1999; "Terrorist Tactics & Counters," and "The Great Martial Art Bodyguard". *Fighting Stars, Black Belt, Grappling, Inside Karate,* and 12th ASLET International Training Seminar "Bagpipe" Rescue Down Officer, Massad Ayoob's Contact Distance Gun Defense Tactics, 1999; Perry William Kelly's *The Man, The Teacher, The Artist (1999),* about Dan Inosanto.

Some of the other articles I have appeared in are: Jerry Beasley's "In Search of the Ultimate Martial Art"; Master Instructor Massad Ayoob's, "The Semi Automatic Pistol in Police Service and Self Defense"; and *Karate Illustrated's,* "On the Road Training.

Two books about *Within Arms Reach are* in progress.

Videos

"Within Arm's Reach" (Volume 1)
Protective Assault Control Locks and Takedowns.
"Within Arm's Reach" (Volume 2)
Close Quarter Defense and Basic Unarmed Hostage Retrieval.
"Within Arm's Reach" (Volume 3)
Teaching Pressure Point Strikes and Combinations for Elite Professionals to aid in Stunning, Controlling, Numbing and Knocking Out Attackers.
"W.A.R." (Volumes 1-15)
Professional and Elite series with Unique Publications/Video.

Professional Memberships

My professional memberships are in accordance with my training. I am a member of the American Teachers of Martial Arts, the American Society of Law Enforcement Trainers, the International Bodyguard Association, and the

Dedication

THE BEGINNING: To my grandparents, Roy and Anna, who encouraged me to learn, love and be the best I could be.

THE PRESENT: To my parents, Josie and Bill. Although they have passed on, I thank them for their unselfishness and sacrifice in providing me with the best education possible. Also for showing me the importance of working for what I want and for teaching me that doing what is right is not always easy.

THE FUTURE: To my sons, Wesley, Wynton and Christopher. May they learn and use the knowledge from the past for the present so they can reach out and touch and live their dreams.

Testimonials

"I recently had the opportunity to attend, what may be, the best thought-out Defensive Tactics Program for Law Enforcement Officers. Mr. Cliff Stewart has developed a program entitled Within Arm's Reach (W.A.R.) after years of research and development with the martial arts as well as law enforcement defensive tactics. The Basic W.A.R. Instructors program was the hardest and most fulfilling program that I had ever undertaken. Mr. Stewart took the opportunity to answer my questions and provided me with the needed "hands-on" time necessary to succeed both on and off duty. It is indeed a "good thing" when we, as law enforcement professionals, are given a total program of defense and then are able to apply these tactics to arrest and control procedures that may be used on duty. In an environment where differing martial arts are being used to accomplish the arrest and control of our suspects throughout the United States, it was indeed a pleasure to see the "why" behind our techniques. I was also given the opportunity to examine and apply pressure point applications within the techniques. I have absolutely no hesitation in recommending this course and Mr. Cliff Stewart, to any professional in the Law Enforcement community who is interested in what may be the finest, holistic, Defensive Tactics Program available."

Captain Dennis Webb
Prince Williams-Manassas
Adult Detention Center
Manassas, Virginia Owner:
Commonwealth Training
Consultants

"Recently, I had an opportunity to attend one of Cliff Stewart's classes. The word that most closely describes his presentation is "AWESOME." The man is the "Godzilla" of tactical defense. His methods are simplistic, easily applied and very effective. I have implemented his techniques into my law enforcement training."

F.M. Becker
DeKalb County Police S. W.A. T. Team
Police Training Academy PO.S. T
Instructor

"I recently was involved as a student in Cliff Stewart's three-day class. As a police officer I am always looking for new skills in defense. The arts that Cliff is teaching are very practical. They really work on the street. Since his class, I have been involved in numerous situations where I used the skills I was taught very successfully. I found Cliff himself to be a very dedicated instructor and I was able to learn more from him in three days than in my 11 years as a police officer."

Eric T. Edmondson
DeKalb County Police S. W.A. T. Team

"As a law enforcement trainer and former military instructor, I believe that Cliff Stewart's W.A.R. concepts are some of the best defensive tactics I have been exposed to. In 11 years I have participated and instructed many defensive tactics programs. Cliff's innovative approach stands head and shoulders above the rest. His theories on physical control are very easy to adapt. I believe that every law enforcement officer who is exposed to daily conflict can learn from Cliff's teachings."

Robert L. Farley Instructor in
Corporate Security;
Executive Protection;
Sniper/Counter Sniper fir the Institute
in Public Service Former Senior
Instructor fir the U.S. Army Protective
Services School

"In less than four hours of training, I was able to restrain and control a subject who was much larger than I was, with confidence. This is the best and easiest defensive tactics course for a woman to learn due to Cliff's ability to communicate his Within Arm's Reach system to me."

*Cpl. Cindy Lee Team
3 Leader with
The Tactical Response Team
Prince Williams-Manassas
Adult Detention Center*

"This was, by far, the most educational Defense Tactics Instructors course I have ever had the pleasure of participating in and I've been involved in the criminal justice field for over 27 years.

Cliff's knowledge and understanding of pressure points completely astounded those in attendance. Cliff's ability to communicate his knowledge and understanding by using his symbols was utterly fantastic.

I would recommend Cliff Stewart's W.A.R. program to everyone involved in the criminal justice field. I'll go even further than that; I would take my annual leave and spend my own money to attend his W.A.R. program."

*Lt. Sonny Alice Prince Williams-
Manassas Adult Detention Center
QIC Tactical Response Team Internal
Affairs/Compliance Officer General
Instructor Tactical Instructor*

"I have just finished reviewing a tape of Cliff Stewart's W.A.R. program. Mr. Stewart did an outstanding job of explaining the complex science of acupuncture points as applied to self-defense scenarios. His approach was both unique and easy to learn. This will prove to be a great asset to both the martial artist and law enforcement communities. I would like to recommend this program to anyone interested in the art of self-defense."

*Grandmaster Rick Moneymaker
9th-Degree Black Belt, Okinawan
Kenpo Founder of the Torte
System*

Mr. Clifford Stewart:

"The Montgomery County Police Tactical Section would like to express our appreciation for the two-day Within Arm's Reach (W.A.R.) seminar presented by you. The techniques and concepts demonstrated improved our offensive/defensive tactics currently employed by our unit. The course validated the direction of our current tactics and streamlined our training by eliminating some stumbling blocks.

Several of our attending personnel are Defensive Tactics Instructors and are practitioners of various other martial arts systems. The concepts taught will improve our training at many different levels.

Hopefully, Mr. Stewart, our tactical section will have the privilege of training with you again in the near future. We would like the opportunity to attend the one-week certification course that we discussed previously.

Thank you again for your time and knowledge."

*The M. C.P Tactical Section
Special Operations Division
Tactical Section*

"If you are a martial artist, if you are in law enforcement, public or private security, or you're just someone looking to acquire skills to help protect you and your loved ones, then I recommend the innovative, comprehensive system of Master Professor Clifford Stewart called W.A.R.

I have personally known and watched him develop W.A.R. (Within Arm's Reach) over the last 33 years and can give personal testimony to the process that he has developed a unique, and more importantly, workable martial arts system. I have seen his untiring efforts and dedication as he has searched for and found the answers to real problems associated with the reality of fighting and self-defense.

And because I was there near the beginning, I know his personal motivation comes from his personal commitment, love of, and to the arts over the years. I have watched this man commit himself tirelessly to not only the arts but to the community and fellow man, reaching out as few ever do.

This man is one of the few that I can honestly say is an absolute expert in his field with few, if any, peers. While others are teaching you skills that have no real application in the real world, Professor Stewart has refined his approach while actually working in the field as an internationally known and recognized personal protector for the rich and poor, the famous and not-so famous, most of his adult life. While others are showing you the rituals of the martial arts, Professor Stewart has refined and taken his survival skills to the max and created applications that can benefit anyone regardless of occupation, age, or physical skill.

I have never given an endorsement in the martial arts or public, private personal protection. I am very proud to do so for the first time in my recommendation of W.A.R. Concepts."

(This letter was written by Ron Chapel, a 10th-degree black belt in American kenpo and executive director of the Ed Parker Institute in Los Angeles, Calif. He is also a public law enforcement veteran of 27 years who has worked on the local, state and federal level. While working as a police officer with the L.A. School District, he and Professor Stewart worked with inner-city youth and gangs. While working as a California State police protective services agent protecting the governor and Chief Justice of the State Supreme Court, he served as a Defensive Tactics Instructor and department academy liaison to the Los Angeles County Sheriff Academy. In addition, he has protected witnesses as a Special Deputy U.S. Marshall for the U.S. Justice Department and served as an Advanced Officer Instructor for the Rio Hondo Police Academy in Southern California.)

The Protectors

Protectors protect lives. It is not a job for anyone or a job everyone can do. There are a number of different types and levels of Protectors. Here are a few rules of thumb every prospective Protector should consider.

- Become a working protection professional before you decide to give up your day job, time, money and sweat.
- Understand the responsibility for protecting lives is a serious one, especially when the sacrifice of your own life may be involved.

Here are some questions to ask yourself as you get started.

1. Are you ready to work long hours under difficult conditions, travel to far-away places, spend lengthy periods of time away from your home and your loved ones?
2. Can you work with different types and kinds of people and cultures?
3. Are you willing to learn all the skills needed to provide the best protective services possible and maintain these skills?
4. Can you be discreet about your clients' business, shortcomings and personal life?
5. Will you refrain from committing any of the following personal protection deadly sins that most assuredly will get you fired.
    a. "They are so rich they don't need this item. I'll just take it."
    b. "I'll just tell them I know about this."
    c. "Why is everyone else so stupid?"
    d. "I'm also right."
    e. "I don't have to do it their way. I got a better way even though I just got here."
    f. "Everybody is on his own. I'm just here for myself."

If you allow any of these sins to become part of your daily routine, you won't be working long in this word-of-mouth world.

The following are a comparison of the many types of Protectors. Also provided is general information regarding training and support.

UNCLE GUARDS — Any relative or friend who will call when he is out of work and in need of extra cash. They have no real desire to be a professional or do any long-term work. If you are lucky they may have some military experience. They will say they used to do martial arts of some kind but they can't remember the style or instructor. They only have a loyalty to themselves. They may have a gun somewhere around the house but can't remember the last time they fired it or cleaned it.

The first thing they want to know is the salary, followed by their days off. They feel if they show up it makes them a bodyguard. How hard could it be?

BUDDY GUARD — Selected because of their friendship and loyalty — which is good place to start — but most of the time that's as far as it goes. Making them different from the "Uncle Guard" is that in the beginning they have desire and sometimes they do a good basic job of security. But most times they just don't know what to do when a situation arises. Instead of taking the path of least resistance, they start by shouting and staring at people to intimidate them. Next comes trying to push people around. Finally comes fighting. And when they get tired of working, they become part of the crowd, rather than the arm trying to control the crowd.

SECURITY GUARDS — People who want to work in the fields of Protection or law enforcement but lack the necessary requirements to gain entrance. Maybe they have yet to test for the position or maybe they failed the test and are waiting to take it again.

Most of the time, however, they're just warm bodies being paid to watch buildings, homes or offices. They may have some training — ranging from eight hours or less at the low end to 40-plus hours at the high end. Their training should include pepper spray, baton, the legal use of force, incident and report writing, first-aid and firearms. Those with this advanced level of training and desire have a firm base in which to help them climb the Protective ladder.

BODYGUARDS — People with a desire to work full time in the protection field. They have some training and in a majority of cases have some attributes or expertise in certain areas such as marital arts, firearms or body building. They may have some on-the-job training but they can only work with certain clientele. In the end, they can provide protection at better than basic level.

LAW GUARDS — Law enforcement personnel who sometimes moonlight as protectors to earn extra money. They carry a firearm and a badge. They can also get some support from other law enforcement agencies. They have good training in how to arrest the bad guys. But therein lies the problem and why many law enforcement personnel make bad CPA's: Their training, mindset and focus is to confront and apprehend people who are breaking the law or people who are about to commit a crime in their presence. Under penalty of law they must respond to the threat or risk losing their job.

However, a CPA's primary responsibility is target denial, which is diametrically opposed to what police officers are taught. A CPA is hired to protect his client's life first and foremost. Law guards will protect the law first and then a client. But thank goodness there are exceptions to this rule. I've worked with some of the best CPA's and Archangels who also were law enforcement officers. The difference is that they also had training in personal protection methods and physical intervention skills beyond their basic law enforcement academy instruction.

PROFESSIONAL (CPA's) — People who had the desire and commitment to select the field of personal protection and who have trained exclusively for VIP protection work. They are fulltime professionals in the area of Protection, they maintain high degrees of physical fitness and keep all firearms and required licenses current.

THE ELITE PROFESSIONAL/ARCHANGEL — The highest of all personal Protectors. In the Christian faith the Archangel was the protector of Heaven and God and the mightiest warrior in creation. The EP or Elite Professional not only possesses the highest physical intervention skills, but he also trains the trainer, commands the teams, heads a company's security division, speaks more than one language, works with a variety of clients all over the world, and has an international network of protection Professionals and lower-level security contacts to support any mission he captains. He can get a room, a reservation, a plane or a boat at a moment's notice.

If you'd like to work in this profession, or are currently working as a Protector in some capacity, you must determine how far you want to go and what you would be willing to do to get there. Be honest with yourself and decide how much commitment you'll be willing to make.

he Protectors Chart

FEDERAL GOVERNMENT

PROTECTORS	REQUIREMENTS	POLITICAL BASE	TRAINING STANDARDS	SPECIFIC PROTECTION TRAINING	SPECIAL POWERS
CIA	Graduate from the Academy		Yes	Yes	Yes
FBI	Graduate from the Academy	Hostages, Foreign Diplomats	Yes	Yes	Yes
SECRET SERVICE	Test, Interview Graduate from the Academy	President and his family; Ex-President and his family, Congress, other visiting world leaders	Yes	Yes	Yes
U.S. MARSHALL	Test, Interview Graduate from the Academy	Criminals, civilians fearing for their lives; Witness Protection	Yes	Witness Protection	Yes

STATE GOVERNMENT

SHERIFF	Test, Interview Graduate from the Academy	Witness; Judge	Yes	No	Yes

FEDERAL GOVERNMENT

MARSHALL/ DEPUTY	Test, Interview Graduate from the Academy	Judges, Witnesses in Court	Yes	Yes	Yes
S.W.A.T.	Test, Interview Graduate from the Academy	Support all other Protectors	Yes	Some	Yes
H.R.T.	Test, Interview Graduate from the Academy Advance	Same as S.W.A.T.	Yes	Some	Yes

EQUIPMENT

SUPPORT OPTIONS	EQUIPMENT	LOCATION OF THE WORK	CLIENT BASE
Yes	Automobiles Other Vehicles Airplanes, Weapons	Worldwide	
Yes	Automobiles Other Vehicles Airplanes, Weapons	Worldwide	
Yes	Local P.O. Limited	U.S.A.	Witnesses, Criminals
Yes	Automobiles Other Vehicles Airplanes, Weapons	U.S.A.	Political
Yes	Limited	Local/City	Court Witnesses
Yes	Limited	Local/City	Court Witnesses
Equipment Local	Expanded	Local/City	Support Witnesses, Judges, Secret Service, FBI
Local Police	Expanded	City	Support S.W.A.T. when necessary

FEDERAL GOVERNMENT

PROTECTORS	REQUIREMENTS	POLITICAL BASE	TRAINING STANDARDS	SPECIFIC PROTECTION TRAINING	SPECIAL POWERS
S.O.R.T.	Test, Interview Graduate from the Academy Advance	Prison Officers, Government Visitors	Yes	Some	Yes
S.E.R.T.	Test, Interview Graduate from the Academy Advance	Prison Officers, Government Visitors	Yes	Some	Yes

PRIVATE

UNCLE GUARDS	None	None	None	None	None
BUDDY GUARDS	None	None	None	None	None
SECURITY	Yes	None	None	Maybe	None
BODYGUARDS	Yes	None	Personal Training	Yes, VIP School, books, On-the-job training	None
LAW GUARDS	Yes	Yes	Yes	Maybe	Yes
CPAs	Yes				
ELITE PROFESSIONALS/ ARCHANGELS	Yes	Yes	Yes	Yes	None

EQUIPMENT

SUPPORT OPTIONS	EQUIPMENT	LOCATION OF THE WORK	CLIENT BASE
Yes	Expanded	Prison	
Yes	Expanded	Prison	
None	Maybe	Location of relative	Whomever
Money	Maybe	U.S.A. Worldwide	Entertainment, friends
Other guards	Yes	Local	Whomever
Team or 911	Yes	U.S.A. Worldwide	All
Local Police	Yes	Local	Off-duty
	Whatever one brings to the table		
Himself	Yes	Worldwide	All

The Foundation

W.A.R. is built on a foundation of the Three-Way Partnership, which includes the unification of mental, physical, and psychological elements. By managing all three elements, we maximize the way we protect others and ourselves. In our quest to achieve this management we sometimes fall short of our goals for a number of reasons. They include a lack of commitment, desire or courage. Commitment constitutes a continued effort until the task or assignment is complete or has failed. Desire is a passion or need to accomplish a particular mission, goal, life statement, task or dream. Courage is performing despite the danger of possible physical, mental, social and psychological harm.

The mental element includes the gathering of data and information as well as the way things should be structured. It also includes an understanding of the goals and options available at the Elite levels. Concentration plays an integral part in our world and requires focusing one's attention on the problems and steps needed to reach a solution. Confidence, the first cousin of courage, can be developed and reinforced through proper training. W.A.R.riorship is the wherehouse of courage and confidence; its storage fee is a code of conduct and a strong commitment toward the value of your life as well as the lives you agree to protect. Instinct control involves managing distractions; it is achieved by understanding the elements of protection training, concentration and awareness. Here is one exercise that will help develop and insure preparedness and alertness:

> "The last thing you want is to start playing catch-up under the threat of assault."

PASSIVE VISUALIZATION: This is practiced in a quiet place with low lighting. This is where you prepare yourself to mentally work through a particular mission or protection problem. For example, I'm walking with my client on Rodeo Drive in Beverly Hills. As we turn the corner we see a man holding a gun on a woman. What options do you have? While lying on your back, eyes closed, breathe in through your nose and fill your stomach with air. Let it rise easily and then blow it out slowly through your mouth, allowing your stomach to return to normal.

Continue this process until the 15-to-20 minute session is complete. Plan to work through one protective problem and as many of the "what-ifs"[1] scenarios you can identify. Please don't rush through the process; taking your time will enhance and reinforce elements of your internal development. By programming the mind to identify environmental clues, you will develop better concentration skills. Your reaction time will be lower and your mindset issues will be affirmed by seeing yourself react positively to specific situations.

This technique allows me to keep sharp under "real" world problems, which is especially valuable when working in the field allows only brief amounts of training time. Don't be fooled into thinking that just because you're lying down relaxed on your back that this mental workout is a snap. If done correctly, this mental workout can be taxing. But it should help you stay on top of your game. The last thing you want is to start playing catch-up when under the threat of assault.

ACTIVE VISUALIZATION — This is where the mental and physical bonding is put into practice in the Pre-Assault stage and prepares you for meeting the conflict aimed at yourself or your client. The mental and breathing processes remains the same. However, a new element is brought into play when movement is coordinated with the mind's solutions to protect your client or control attacks.

Try to find a room that provides ample space for movement. Some people prefer a quiet room. But I like to put on some music by James Brown, The Eagles or Will Smith. I choose music that will boost my energy level and help develop my movement concentration skills before I go out on assignment. If I'm going to sleep or about to prepare for tomorrow's mission, I choose music with a slower tempo to promote slower breathing and movements.

As you start the exercise, lock your door to prevent unwanted visitors. If you can, turn off your phone. However, when you're on duty, keep the lines of communication open at all times. Begin by picking a "what-if" problem. Choose one problem at a time and breathe through your nose, letting your stomach rise on all pulling motions. Now exhale through your mouth and let your stomach return to normal. Whenever there's cause to strike, draw your weapon with a push or pull move very, very, very slowly. Most people make the mistake of moving too fast at first. Start slow and then increase your speed as you become more comfortable and confident. It's always better to be "correct" over "fast". Think of the options that will provide the best solutions. This is a protective kata (a martial arts term for a form). By doing these visualization exercises, you can increase your muscle and mental reaction time. The above mental processes will provide you with the tools and choices to gather information.

The psychological element involves the management of emotions. Fear is the response to a real or unreal incident that triggers a number of physical, mental and psychological reactions. When fear is experienced, the brain triggers its survival tools and instantly sends epinephrine, norepinephrine and endorphin into your body from the endocrine system. Your survival tool invokes super painkillers.

Your heart rate, blood pressure and respiration work to free and increase oxygen to the blood to help with the intense and prolonged anger. The need to fight (physical intervention) or flight (target denial) aid in your survival. Your tool bag switches the brain into hyper-drive and brings up all files on survival and options learned from your training; the data is being processed so fast that it may actually feel like you're slowing down. This phenomena is known as tachypsychia, meaning from the speed of the mind. Now your pre-assault training takes over. The thousands of correct repetitions, periods of meditation, passive and active visualization enhance what physiologists call longterm muscle memory. Your response to an attack is automatic, one that takes place under subconscious rather than conscious command. Sometimes it occurs at such speed the conscious mind can't keep up.

At the Elite Level, you may feel as though there are two of you: a passive spectator and an active combatant. Massad Ayoob, one of my Master Instructors and the person who wrote the foreword to this book, calls this effect psychological splitting. His intensive and on-going research with survivors of deadly force attacks finds that the more highly and correctly trained you are, the more likely a mini-you and maxi-you will appear when push comes to shove.

An instant shot of mind-produced adrenaline makes you more powerful but also clumsier. Enhanced muscle activity may cause muscle tremors. That shaking feeling you experience is another reaction of adrenaline. It is also because of a symptom called vaso-construction, which is an increase of blood flow to major muscle groups. This reduces feeling in the extremities, making fine motor skills more difficult to perform.

It is better to use more exaggerated movements under these conditions. Psychologically, this emotional turmoil creates a struggle among the Three-Way Partnership. You may know what to do mentally, but certain outside stimuli can slow or freeze physical intervention techniques. Another side effect is what I call mental removal, where you wish you were somewhere safer, whether it be at home with your loved ones or as far from the situation as possible. I call this mental flight.

Another emotional side effect is hoping that something or someone will intercede. You are now in what I call "stalled" and have placed both you and your client in great danger. This factor most often occurs among those who are either untrained or are incorrectly trained.

> "It's always better to be correct than fast."

Fear Management is understanding the fear response and directing and applying these responses to your training, planning, mindset and physical intervention tactics and strategy. When a fight-or-flight incident occurs, you know it is a sign of strength, speed, power and high resistance to pain and you are supercharged.

Grandmaster Joe Lewis, former World Heavyweight Kickboxing Champion and the father of American kickboxing, is considered to be one of the greatest full-contact fighters of all time. He also is a master of organization combative science. He taught that mental drifting or stalling in a fight/assault is caused by not having a point of view (plan, method or program) or incorrect training. Another expert, Grandmaster Jerry Smith, trainer of over a dozen kickboxing champions and the designer of the five-level method of Martial Science and Self-Defense, shared his concept of Present Focus based on working your program's principles like the principles of Within Arm's Reach with the flow of the fight/assault. This helps you remain in the present. Also needed is a strong physical and mental conditioning method that exploits the fear responses, while combining a strong principle base method and a Warrior mindset. A W.A.R. mindset constitutes the mental, physical and emotional acceptance of a particular course of action.

Ego Management is the skill of not allowing what others think of you to get in the way. This is also a part of target denial: You cannot allow your ego to become a factor in predictability.

Psychological Management is the skill of governing actions influenced by emotional factors and elements. Most of the time we make emotional choices out of frustration. This is because of training which fails to teach good awareness techniques or forces you to have less time to analyze information, formulate plans or implement physical intervention options before and during a conflict.

AWARENESS
"The Casino"

Las Vegas, Nev. — Larry Flynt, owner and publisher of *Hustler* magazine, avoids serious injury when a lone gunman attempts to...

It was 3:45 a.m. and the thermometer was still pushing the 90-degree mark. Another sweltering desert summer night that had turned into early morning. A Las Vegas casino was almost barren except for about ten small rollers split up at two tables just outside the special section reserved for high rollers in the rear of the room. At the high-rollers section, Larry Flynt, Amarillo Slim, Pudgy, The Kid and two other gamblers were playing seven card stud, wild jacks or better.

The game had been going on for at least 12 hours, which was the amount of time the three of us had been on duty. We tried to stay alert for potential problems, but boredom was creeping in. As Director of Security for Larry Flynt, my primary duty was to maintain Personal Awareness (PA). This principle is the basis for all the other elements needed to survive as a Close Protection Agent (CPA). Mr. Flynt had already received a number of death threats, and alleged contracts on his life were still in force, so our job was more than just to keep the gawkers and curious away.

With the help of the casino's security staff, we had developed a three-layered protective circle around the high-roller's section where Larry's game was taking place. The first line of defense would be the outer ring composed of four of the casino's uniformed guards, who stood about 20 yards from our table.

The middle ring was formed by three of the casino's undercover security agents. The first agent was assigned to the slot machines. Another positioned herself at the bar, where she was drinking double shots of cranberry juice and 7-up, while maintaining a clear view of our table. The last agent was placed at one of the black jack tables so she could observe the activity and maintain radio contact with all other agents. All three were about ten-to- 12 yards from our section.

The inner circle was Larry's team, which contained three CPAs. The first was Bill, an ex-Marine Force Recon Vietnam vet with 35 years of service under his belt. The second agent was Phil, a 26-year-old strong, bright and highly skilled marksman from Bakersfield, Calif. In addition to the training both men brought to the table, they were students of Within Arm's Reach and had been trained by me for approximately seven months. The third agent was I, Clifford Stewart, Director of Security for Larry Flynt for the past year and a half.

As part of our strategy, we changed positions every 20-to-45 minutes in a random pattern to provide familiarity with all zones, not to be fixed targets, and to keep 360-degree coverage at all times. Because of our close proximity to each other, we used hand signals and maintained radio communications with the casino's agents. I was scanning my zone of responsibility when six people entered through the back door. Three were "biker" types. They wore jeans and vests and revealed arms that

Cliff guarding Larry Flynt, who can be seen in the right corner of this photograph.

were heavily tattooed. Each of the bikers either held a beer or a silver dollar. As they entered the casino, they looked and pointed in our direction. After we made eye contact with the group, they turned, laughed among themselves, and went back outside.

Next to where the bikers had been standing was a couple in their 60s wearing matching "Viva Las Vegas" T-shirts, brown shorts, white socks and tennis shoes. They briefly glanced our way, then focused on the "One-Arm Bandits." With cups of coins in their hands, they stationed themselves at their slot machines.

To the rear of the middle-aged couple, steadily moving in and out of view, was a young man wearing a white jacket. He had both hands in his pockets and was looking at the floor. He moved quickly behind a group of slot machines. At this point, the outer and middle rings focused on the bikers. The uniformed security ran outside after the bikers, while undercover agents scurried toward the back door to pick up anything happening outside.

My team and I picked up on the man in the white jacket, who was now moving in a circle. His back was against the wall, lurking in the shadows. With hand signals, Bill, Phil and I confirmed we were on the same page.

From the three months of training in our Pre-Assault Training sessions, we used Plan 2, which entailed the agent closest to the restroom pretending to enter the facilities. I was that agent, so I made it look like I was going to the restroom, but in reality I was trying to inconspicuously get behind this guy.

My team let me know the suspect had given them a couple of quick looks, then pushed his hand down again into his pocket. He started to move slowly back toward the rear door. Then suddenly, he turned, looked at the table and fixed his eyes on Larry. At that point, he began to move straight toward the table. The team moved into position to obstruct any direct line of sight between the man in the white jacket and Larry, the possible target.

He never noticed me approaching. When I was four yards away, I glanced at the team. Phil rubbed his nose, which meant he and Bill were good to go. The undercover units were ready and I had the green light. When I was one step from the guy, I "bolstered the Colt". I took a deep breath and leaped, He didn't notice me until I touched his right wrist and elbow. He tried to turn toward me but I pulled him 90 degrees across my shoulder line to take his balance, and to control the weapon that I suspected was in his jacket pocket.

While holding onto him I looked at him and I asked, "Can I help you?" He said, "No, what's the problem?"

"What's in your pocket?" I asked. "Nothing," he said, as he lifted hard on his right hand to free it from his pocket. At that point, I hit his center triceps and pulled down hard on his wrist. His hand ripped through the lining of the jacket and a .32-caliber pistol fell to the ground. With a hammer back, I swept him backward as I yelled, "Gun!" The CPA's moved Larry to our safe room, while the other rings of protection moved in to help. I scanned for others who could be involved, but it was clear.

We learned later that the man in custody wanted to become famous, no matter what it took, no matter what the cost.

> "Mr. Flynt had already received a number of death threats, and alleged contracts on his life were still in force."

AWARENESS- The Super Principle of WITHIN ARM's REACH

Awareness is the First Principle, the father Principle, the Super Principle of Personal Protection Defense, family defense and client protection. Awareness is the foundation of Within Arm's Reach (W.A.R.) and for all the skills, tactics and physical intervention applications taught. I emphasize the development of Awareness skills to maximize protecting yourself and others.

This was just one of many attempts made against Larry Flynt during the four years I worked as his Director of Security. What made it nothing more than an attempt was our ability to recognize a problem before it happened and deal with it in an efficient manner.

This incident illustrates the use of three vital concepts: Awareness, Pre-Assault Training, and Teamwork.

Awareness is a two-step process. The first step is to define awareness. "Awareness is the measure of personal preparedness that determines your alertness, perception and understanding of your internal alarms, environmental clues and indicators."

People always say, "Be alert," "be aware," "be careful out there," but rarely are you shown how to be alert, aware and careful.

The second step is knowing the two types of awareness needed in the personal protection business. First is personal or Internal Awareness. The second is Environmental or External awareness. Let's look at each type.

Personal Awareness

WHITE ZONE — The use of the color-code concept made famous by Jeff Copper. The first color zone is the White Zone. In the White Zone, a person is most vulnerable to attack because he is usually completely absorbed in some other activity such as a game, conversation or day-dreaming.

If you are attacked when you are in the **White Zone,** your chances of reacting fast enough are low or non-existent altogether.

YELLOW ZONE — **The Yellow Zone** represents caution. For example, you are walking to your car and you notice two men, one with his back to you and the other looking to his right and avoiding eye contact. You now have time to respond if necessary.

ORANGE ZONE — **The Orange Zone** represents a need to be alert. Now, those same men start to move away from each other and toward your direction. Neither are looking at you. Thinking this could be trouble, you go into primary response mode.

RED ZONE — Red means physical confrontation. Because you didn't get your keys into your car door fast enough, you're now being pulled from your car.

BLACK ZONE — Some people use this as a fight for your life, but I think by this time, you are either controlling the conflict or losing the battle.

The secrets of Awareness, however, goes far beyond color codes, cues or sounds. You must be thinking in the "here and now". You must be in the present. These types of Awarenesses necessitate a strong foundation.

The first step to mastery is meditation, which will clean, clear, prepare and refuel your focus centers. I teach the Quantum Flow method by George Quant. It's easy, direct and effective.

The second step is to turn on your computer (your mind) and begin to think in terms of personal protection. I use the 12-6-3-9 method; that is, I see my environment as a clock. I look at what is in the front (12), back (6) and on each side of me (9 and 3) and ask myself if I'm ready to employ my physical intervention skills.

The third step is visualization, of which there are two types. The first type is passive visualization, where you find a quiet place with low lights and mentally work through as many "what-ifs" as possible. This allows me to perform under real-life situations with only a small about of training. Don't kid yourself: This can be a heavy mental workout when done correctly.

The second type of visualization is active visualization, where the mental and physical bonding occurs in the Pre-Assault stage. The mental process remains the same, but now movement is coordinated with the mind. You need a quiet room with space to freely move. Pick a hypothetical problem, then move and think of as many options as possible to provide protection. This is a protective kata, which programs the proper response during a conflict. It cuts down on your reaction time, reinforces a proper point of view, and encourages the proper mindset elements and W.A.R.riorship attitude. Of course, this doesn't replace real physical training, but it will enhance your training a great deal, while serving to support and improve your management skills in terms of psychological control factors.

AWARENESS DESTRUCTION
Controlling People's Minds

One aspect that will take you out of the protection awareness game is failing to control your emotions. The fear element manifests itself if you are preoccupied with any type of loss, injury or social position. It is an Ego Management problem if shame or embarrassment keeps you from performing at the top of your game. Wondering about what to do (Mindset) or whether you'll do the right thing (Pre-Assault) will almost always guarantee failure. When these elements are not managed, it will affect your ability to detect cues and physical indications that help protect yourself and others. Professional environmental awareness is identifying physical and audio cues through a "sixth sense" about the environment.

ENVIRONMENTAL INDICATORS AND CUES

PHYSICAL INDICATORS — Environmental opportunities that can provide a launching pad for assaults.

Lighting or lack of it affects vision. Depending on the position of the sun, it can either blind you (be in your eyes) or aid you (be at your back). The time of day — whether the sun is rising or setting — may help decide your plan of action and what equipment is needed. If it's nighttime, is there moonlight? And is there a full moon, halfmoon or quarter-moon? What about street lighting? You need to know the type of lighting, the number on each side of the street and how closely positioned they are to each other. It is best to avoid dark alleys, hallways and poorly lit rooms.

Try to avoid these "traps" at all costs; but sometimes, however, you have no choice but to proceed. In these cases, having the right equipment can make all the difference in the world. Helping to eliminate the cloak of darkness are Mini Mag lights, night vision goggles or scopes.

Openings

Another indicator of potential trouble can be found with doors, windows or gates that are neither completely opened nor closed. They provide an attacker with concealment, as well as easier audio and visual access to your movements.

AUDIO

Sound can be an indicator, whether it's loud, quiet or eerily still. A sign of trouble can be when people are whispering and glancing at you at the same time. It's not hard to recognize a potential problem when someone is shouting at you or your client, but remember it could only be a distraction for an attack from a different angle.

OBSTRUCTIONS

Obstructions come in the form of trucks, automobiles or barricades placed in a certain pattern that forces your driver to alter his predetermined route.

BODY LANGUAGE

Reading a person's body language can provide cues and help you identify potential problems. Beware of someone totally still or in a "freeze" position. If a person is agitated, you might see him rub his hands together while making hard and jerky movements. Or he may unwittingly assume a fighting stance similar to boxing or karate. This is an indication he may be ready to run, jump or hit. Next, look for someone shifting or rocking his body back and forth, sometimes being seen in conjunction with conversations being carried on with imaginary friends or foes. Another cue is clenched fists combined with shoulder shifting, head dropping, or knees bending or locking. This may be a sign that an attack is imminent.

The eyes can be cues to a person's intent or will. Here's what to look for:

THE STARE

A person with a 1,000-mile stare seems to be looking mindlessly into the distance, but in fact is trying to disguise great internal stress and conflict, which could present itself through an overt act of violence at any moment. This usually occurs before...

THE GLARE

Glaring is focused attention at one or more people. It's as if the suspect had X-ray vision and was trying to intimidate you.

THE GLANCE

First comes the "sizing up", a quick look to determine whether the victim is an easy target. Next comes the "set-up", a glance that combines conversation with you or another person. There is a second of stillness to look the target up and down followed by scanning of the area for something that might stop them.

THE TARGET GLANCE

This is a quick peek at the place or person he is about to hit.

THE "I'M-GOING-FOR-IT" GLANCE

This occurs when he takes a quick look at you. Then he will take a step away, his head will drop, the shoulders will raise and the weight will shift to the foot farthest from you. Next, he will turn and take a quick target glance as he strikes either by jumping or extending the front leg.

THE HANDS

The hands can be used to hurt or kill, but so can the feet when the perpetrator is trained. Watch to see whether the hands are in position to go for a weapon.

Target Denial and Physical Intervention "Dining with Mr. T"

I was having an early dinner with "A-Team" legend, Mr. T at the famous Palms restaurant in West Hollywood, Calif., one evening. We were competing to see who could eat the biggest steak. We ordered identical dinners: a 32-ounce, well-done steak, salad, corn and rolls, not to mention the best, and I mean, the best lemonade money could by.

I had been Mr. T's Close Protection Agent (CPA) for the past two years. I was the latest in a long line of security types employed by the actor (See the chapter on "The Protectors"); all of my predecessors had lost their jobs because they committed one or more of the "deadly sins".

While we were in mortal combat with the two pounds of beef, corn, salad and bread, I noticed two body-builder types pointing and looking at us through the window. At first I thought it was because they recognized Mr. T, but then they followed with an unflattering gesture and started to flex. I could see trouble coming through the front door.

I got up from my seat, went outside and asked if there was a problem. They said they were, "Going to kick Mr. T's ass and mine too if I got in the way!" These weren't small boys; these guys had arms the size of tree trunks. Now Mr. T and I could counter with 18-inch-plus arms, but these guys were so beefed up they made Mr. T and I look like children. So I said, "Look, I'll be right back with Mr. T, so you'd better warm up and hop up or do whatever you do to get ready for an ass kicking!"

As I was about to go back into the restaurant, I turned to them and said, "Don't go anywhere."

Once back at the table, I told Mr. T about the problem and suggested we pay the bill. I called the limo driver and told him to meet us at the back of the restaurant. The manager allowed us to exit through the kitchen and we quickly got into the limo and drove onto Santa Monica Boulevard. As we passed our challengers, we rolled down the window of the limo and waved. They saw us leaving and began to jump up and down, screaming like little children. Then they started throwing their shirts down on the sidewalk and began running after the limo, yelling that they were going to get us. Twenty yards behind them were the flashing lights of a police car.

Mr. T looked at me and said, "I guess they will be explaining to the police what they were doing while we are on our way home to our ladies."

Also, because of our challengers' timing, we never got to finish dinner, so it's still not known who would have won the steak-off. The principles I used in this situation were: Awareness, both Personal and Active; Target Denial-Primary Response; Ego Management; Exit options (tactics to be used in case of emergencies); and Cover and Concealment options (cover options include objects that will stop bullets, such as telephone poles, fire hydrants, old-fashioned mail boxes, steel car rims and engine blocks. Concealment items include trash bins, large boxes, walls and doors).

Cliff with Mr. T and Larry Hartsell.

Physical Intervention

Physical Intervention applies the principles of the martial sciences to protect ourselves and others by using hand-to-hand combat techniques, weapons, single and team tactics, strategies, legal use of force, medical aid (if needed), and personal sacrifice.

Physical Intervention involves protecting us as well as others. There are several key steps in Physical Intervention tactics:

- **Becoming a physical obstruction between your client and the threat;**

- **Physically removing oneself and others to a safe haven or position, for example a car, house, another city or state. Once removal is accomplished the Target Denial is utilized;**

- **Providing medical aid;**

- **Taking physical control by removing the attacker. To physically control a person, you must know how to weaken his physical structure, mental attitude and when possible, his psychological framework.**

W.A.R. seminar on physically controlling a person.

The Ninja in the Overcoat

The phone rang and my whole body shook. I turned, grabbed the phone and put it to my ear. "Who's calling?" I asked. "This is the hotel's bell captain. I got to let you know a guy asked about Larry and wanted to know if he was here in the hotel."

We were in Columbus, Ohio. Larry Flynt, owner and publisher of *Hustler* magazine, was in town for a lawsuit filed against him by Bob Guccione, owner of *Penthouse* magazine. We had requested police protection because of the large number of death threats Mr. Flynt received on a daily basis. The police said they could not provide protection because of a shortage of manpower, but they would permit Mr. Flynt's Close Protection Agents to carry firearms.

We sent our names over to the court and asked that the list be forwarded to the local police. We wanted to make sure everyone knew it was alright to carry firearms while in town.

A guy asking about Larry Flynt had told a bellhop that if he told him where Larry's room was, there was $20 in it for him. "Cliff," he said, "I took the $20 and told him Larry was in one of the penthouse suites, either on the ninth or the tenth floor, because those were the only floors where there were penthouse suites and I couldn't be sure which one it was."

"The guy said okay and told me to forget about seeing him," he added. "I saw him take the back stairs instead of the elevator."

"How long ago did you see him?" I asked. "About one minute ago. I just took the time to make sure he was gone and I got to glance at the clock on the TV. It was 3:18 a.m."

The bellhop thanked me for the $100 and I added, "You'll get another $100 when I see you."

I put down the phone and was rolling out of bed when the phone rang again. I picked it up and it was security. "Cliff, there is a man coming up the stairs with a long overcoat with what looks like some kind of butt stock hidden under the coat on the right side."

"How can you tell?" I asked.

"Because it looks like the same imprint I see when we go hunting wearing our long raincoats."

"How long ago and what floor was he on?" I asked. "He is on the third floor moving slowly, but checking out everything. He asked me what floor Larry was on and I told him the 9th, at the end of the hall to the right."

"What does he look like?"

"He's about 6-foot-2, 220, white with a beard," said the bellhop.

I continued my roll out of the bed, grabbed the gun, jumped into sweats, jumped back on the bed, and called Larry's room.

Phil answered.

"It's Cliff and we have a storm coming in about five minutes. Button down the ship. "

"Roger that!" he responded. I said, "Larry's asleep, call 911. There is a silent running bad guy in an overcoat. He's 6-foot-2, 220, Caucasian, with a beard and has some long object under his coat. I got it and I'm on it. Let's rock and roll!"

The phone was back on the hook. All this took about 45 seconds. I opened the door on the 10th floor, peeped back and forth and all looked clear for the moment. The outside guard, Taroo, looked at me. He made you crazy with his hands. I signaled for him to come to my room in a hurry. Without a wasted motion, he grabbed a chair, magazine and came into my room.

"A bad guy is coming up the back stairwell with something under his overcoat. We don't know what else he has, but it looks long. Taroo, boy," I said. "That takes a lot of balls. You keep watch and I'm calling the other guys."

I made two more calls — one to Bill and the other to Big Larry. I sent Taroo down to the end of the hall to see when the man in question was coming. The rest of his guys would go back into our room and wait for the signal. The problem was that all our rooms were directly across from each other. If we sandwiched him in the middle, we risked being caught in a crossfire. The plan was that I would take him down and they would provide cover. We could then disarm him and wait for the police to take him away. Well, it sounded fine at the time.

The up-and-coming security guard, who was quickly moving to bodyguard status, had also called 911 and said there was a man with a gun. He advised the police to hurry.

We all got into place and waited for what seemed to be forever. Our doors were closed but our eyes peeked through the peephole, waiting for what I called "Show Time." The moment of truth was approaching — this is where you either earn your money or get hurt trying.

One minute passed, then two, then three, and then I saw him through the peephole. It was the man in a long coat walking slowly in our direction.

Timing is everything. I had to take him just as he passed by my door. It couldn't be too soon because that would give him a chance to react and use his weapon. If I tried to take him after he passed, the same problem could arise. In real life, there are no retakes. I had one chance to do it right.

By now he was six feet away, then five, then four, then three, then two. When he reached the one-foot mark, it was "Show Time!" Taroo pulled open the door and I felt like a skydiver jumping out of an airplane. I blew through the opening just as his right shoulder was in the center of the doorframe. Everything appeared to be going in slow motion. He started to turn and as he did, I slammed a palm heel strike into his forehead. I kept my hand there and broke his vertical plane backward, taking his balance instantly. My right hand had a death grip on his right wrist. I fired a knee to the center of his thigh but connected with steel rather than muscle. I maintained downward pressure on his right arm and forgot about the pain in my knee. Using the knee strike to push his hips out of alignment, I broke his structure and dropped him like a bag of potatoes.

He fell face up but I rolled him over, moved my hand from the front of his head to the rear, slammed his face hard into the carpet and added a hammerfist to the base of his ear as hard as I could. Once face down, he was much easier to control. And if his weapon had discharged, it would have been driven into the carpet rather than being allowed to skip across the ground. A bullet can skip like a rock across placid water if shot at the right angle. All in all, I was in a better position to control him.

I pulled my hand from his wrist to the weapon and it felt like a double-barrel shotgun. I yelled, "Gun, Gun!" I held onto the barrel for dear life but he was not struggling. My team had him covered with its weapons. They wanted to clear the line of fire. I did- , n't want to release the weapon but the point was moot. He was **The moment** out cold.

> **of truth was approaching — you either earn your money or get hurt trying."**

We rolled him over just enough to see the weapon. It was a double-barrel shotgun, sawed off and tied to his wrist. We cut the tape to his wrist and pulled the weapon from his grasp. We opened the shotgun and found shells in both barrels. We placed flex cuffs on him and pulled him into my room. We kept one agent outside to meet the police and another to provide cover in case he wasn't working alone. The others went to Larry's room and bolted the door.

The police arrived at 3:35 a.m. They told everyone to drop their weapons. They questioned us and we told them how everything went down. The bell captain confirmed our story, as did the night watch commander. The police cleared us with the night watch commander, and took our "Ninja in the Overcoat" into custody. By the way, our "Ninja" was a convicted felon, fresh out of prison, and had served time for attempted murder. He never revealed to the police who sent him.

The police returned our weapons and we went back to our rooms. I placed an extra man on duty, while the police placed two men on Larry's floor for the remainder of our stay.

The rest of us held a debriefing meeting to discuss how we could have better handled the situation. We tried to got back to bed but none of us could fall asleep.

Larry didn't wake up until the next day.

This incident illustrates how intelligent reporting, outer rings of protection and PreAssault training and planning, along with close-quarter aggressive defense training and team training, can insure safe personal protection.

The Three Stages of Conflict

Pre-Assault or conflict is the time prior to an incident or conflict. For the professional, it is not a matter of if, but when.

In the world of the Elite Professional, there are specific needs for each category of protector. The elements required for S.W.A.T. or H.R.T. teams are different from that of a SEALs team, the Green Berets or Force Recon Units. They may need similar types of skills, but their applications and levels of force are different. Police department polices concerning use of force are different from the State Department, which are different from CPA's. The primary mission statement of a particular unit may differ greatly because of the varying degrees of objectives. But in general, each unit shares an understanding of the three stages of conflict — Pre-, Present- and Post-Assault. Every elite team will find itself flowing among the stages.

The CPA flow is mostly in a pre-event stage where the individual CPA does preparation and training. When all hell breaks loose there seldom is notification before the event occurs as is often the case when S.W.A.T. or H.R.T. are called to respond to an incident. CPA's only have their states of awareness. Personal and legal survival should be at the top of the Post-Event checklist.

Prep assault is for Prep Time: This includes planning tactics and strategies and correcting past mission mistakes, delegating assignments to agents, and advanced detail work. This is also the time to form the team, discuss client and personal limitations, and active awareness practice. It also marks the time to maintain equipment, repair or acquire new items (i.e., communications systems and supports) and obtain legal updates and use of force issues, policies and applications.

Whatever the call letters — S.W.A.T, H.R.T, S.E.R.T, or S.O.R.T. — they stand in a continuous pre-incident mode of training as required by their department until called to control conflicts and incidents. Most of us return to the pre-incident phase after a conflict, but at the Elite Level this pre-phase can last as little as a few minutes or as long as a few weeks.

This is the time to make note of the legal ramifications of every action your team may consider an option. Elite Professionals spend most of their time developing, maintaining, improving or acquiring new skills in the pre-conflict phrase. Elite Professional teams endure a consent ebb and flow — from training (pre-conflict) to the mission (the event); from post-conflict, debriefing tactics review, and medical treatment to burying the dead and taking time off. Then the pre-phrase strategy begins again.

The Westwood Assault

It was a little after 1 a.m. in Westwood, just about a block from the U.C.L.A. campus. Larry Flynt and his wife, Althea, had been to dinner and a movie. My CPA teammembers included Darrel Carson and Chuck Herd. Carson, who was my supervisor and friend, is one of the toughest and brightest CPAs and private investigators I have ever met. He is a black belt master in shotokan karate and speaks perfect Spanish. Herd, the other Archangel, was a retired Los Angeles Police Department sergeant who had 30 years on the force. Chuck was an exception to the police department rule. He was a tough veteran of the mean streets of south central Los Angeles. He always kept his skills sharp and deadly.

Chuck was driving the trail car. This planet is a little less safe because of his passing, but that night I had Archangels at my side and back. We had good information that there would be an attempt on Mr. Flynt's life soon so we were on full alert with four-man teams armed with shotguns in the follow car. The fourth man on the team was Retired Lt. George Bennet, an L.A.P.D. Homicide Detective. Like Chuck, George was an Archangel of the highest order.

Darrel and I were in a long black limo driven by a young untrained driver who was someone's cousin (an Uncle Guard for sure). We were turning right off Westwood Boulevard when I noticed a dark van parked in an alley. Three men stood outside the van. I looked for weapons, but saw only beer bottles. The van's side door was open and I could see three additional subjects sitting inside.

The ground was dry and the streetlights overhead were casting light downward, which made it difficult to see their faces. We were close to the curb as we turned off Westwood Boulevard. I was sitting up front in the limo in the passenger seat. Darrel, sitting in the middle position, also saw the problem unfolding. Chuck and George called on the hand radio to say the van looked like a possible problem. They also said that the shotguns were ready if we needed them.

The young driver was asked to move to the outside lane, but instead he froze and stopped the car. Darrel took the wheel and tried to turn the car away from the curb. But on our outside was a car whose inhabitants were trying to get close enough to see who was inside the limo. There was also was a car in front of us, slowing down at the alley to look at the men drinking and pushing each other. Darrel blew the horn but the car in front of us continued its snail pace. Darrel got his firearm ready. The follow car kept close to the curb in case it had to provide back-up.

Two of the guys outside the van started walking toward the limo. Darrel had the front of the car in his sight in case this was a trap. I had my weapon out of the holster, ready for the two approaching men. One of the men stopped right in front of the limo. The Uncle Guard driver hit the brakes to keep from running over him.

NEVER, EVER stop a car when there is a possible physical threat unless there is no way out. Although the approaching suspect was unarmed and low on the threat level, I had to respond immediately on a low level of force but be ready to escalate to a higher force level if necessary. I bolstered my weapon, opened the door and jumped out of the limo. I closed the door and yelled to Darrel, "Go, go, go, get out of here now!"

As I ran to the front of the limo, everything seemed to be moving in slow motion. The closer I got to him, the more it seemed as if I was watching someone else in action. The man in front of the limo was huge — about 6-foot-4, 260 pounds and he had his hands on the hood.

"Get out of way!" I yelled. He turned and laughed as I kept moving toward him. His buddy was about ten feet away and dropped his beer bottle, apparently surprised that someone had jumped out of the limo and was challenging his friend. Out of the corner of my right eye I could see that both men's hands were empty. I also caught a glimpse of the others jumping out of the van. When I got close enough to the man whose hands were on the hood of the limo, he stood up, turned and swung at me with his right hand. I parried the punch with my left hand as my right arm lifted up under his punch. I attacked his center triceps. I turned my lift motion into a push, spun him around and used a palm heel strike to the rear of the head to knock him forward onto the sidewalk. He was out cold.

At the same time, Darrel had taken over the driving assignment and tried to get the limo out of the kill zone. The second guy came running at me full speed. I moved toward him to get out the way of the limo and change his attack timing. When he got close, he kicked hard at my groin. I brought up my leg and shin blocked the kick. Then I stepped down and forward and served a kenpo elbow sandwich to his head that put him down and out. I turned to engage the other occupants of the van but Chuck and George had them under control. Their shotguns were trained on the others, who now were all in felony-prone positions. Darrel moved the limo out of the kill zone and was turning the corner when Mr. Flynt demanded the limo stop and wait for me. Against Darrel's better judgment, he acquiesced.

Chuck, George and I jumped into the follow car and radioed for the limo to go. As we got the hell out of there, West L.A.P.D. was called to follow up on the van and its occupants. The limo and follow car went quickly back to Mr. Flynt's Bel-Air estate and I called ahead to alert the home security team to be on full alert following the controlled incident.

Later that night Chuck got information on our attackers: no wants or warrants, no criminal background, two drunk and disorderly charges, one assault charge in a bar fight and the others were clean.

Our Pre-Assault training demanded that anyone involved in a physical intervention event or assault would be left behind if remaining compromised the safety of the client. I asked why they stayed and the older vet said, "You still owe us lunch."

Darrel said he told Mr. Flynt I needed to sign the time sheet. Larry said he doesn't leave his people. Sometimes all the training in the world doesn't work if your team has its own mindset of taking care of each other whenever possible. The assault event is the pass/fail of any elite team and it is a matter of life or death.

The van people were just six intoxicated guys on the town looking for fun and trouble, but it could just have easily been an attack on Larry's life. Darrel thought the entire incident took place in under five minutes.

Once we were engaged in the incident, from moment to moment, we made the correct choices for the level of use of force, target denial options, and physical intervention options.

The assault stage tests and demands using your awareness and physical intervention skills as well as maximizing the Three-Way Partnership concept.

According to Massad Ayoob, the concepts needed to survive an assault are:

1. **Awareness;**
2. **Tool Development;**
3. **Technique Tuning;**
4. **Proper Tactics;**
5. **Combining Techniques and Tactics;**
6. **Correct Choice of Techniques, Tactics and Equipment; and**
7. **The Right Teammembers.**

What Are Your Force Options?

FIRST OPTION: Target Denial

SECOND OPTION: Release yourself or your client from the attacker's grasp.

THIRD OPTION: Lock and control.

FOURTH OPTION: Stun and render unconscious.

FIFTH OPTION: Deadly Force.

YOUR LEGAL OPTIONS
   a. Citizen's Arrest

   b. A lawsuit can be filed against you and/or your client for excessive force.

Post-Assault

In the aftermath of conflict, even though you have survived, the threat is not over because there are number of aspects to be considered.

- Are there any legal ramifications? Have you filed a formal complaint with your local law enforcement department? The law is usually more empathetic to the person who first reports a crime. But before you call, contact you legal counsel and ask him the best way to proceed.

- Are there any criminal issues (i.e., has you or your team been accused of using excessive force)? Have you been arrested for violating a weapon permit?

- Are there civil issues pending against you or your client?

- Have you, members of your team or your clients needed medical attention? What were the medical injuries caused by your attackers? Are their injuries minor, major, life threatening, permanent or fatal?

- Have you embarrassed your client? Did you anger or affect the public by your attitude or actions? Did you cross cultural lines and values? Client approval or disapproval of your tactics and public relation skills are very important and must always be considered.

- If the conflict was not resolved, go back to ground zero and look for the next reoccurrence of the threat.

- Have you considered the possibility that you may be the subject of a revenge threat because you and your team either kept the conflict under control or possibly injured one or more of the attackers.

- Have you and your team held the necessary debriefing so you can improve on the manner in which you handled the assault.

There are other ramifications beyond the legal, medical and social consequences. After surviving physically, one must also be able to survive psychologically. Post-Assault trauma is common and has specific symptoms. After a conflict people may experience emotional mood swings, nightmares, loss of sleep, feelings of guilt and inadequacy or even impotency. These feelings are real and relate to the conflicts you have encountered.

The proper mindset, training and foundation in the W.A.R.riorship concept, coupled with strong psychological management tools, can assist you in surviving the aftermath of an assault. This allows you to return to the Pre-Assault stage better prepared to survive all phases of a conflict.

Hand-to-Hand and Beyond

Within Arm's Reach (W.A.R.) is a multifaceted method of personal defense and protection designed for elite professionals. It can be beneficial to professionals who need to enhance their skills in pre-assault observation, develop their body into an aggressive defensive tool, and teach tactics and strategy for multiple attackers. Also emphasized are impact and edged weapons use; retention tactics that work for any weapon you carry; firearm usage for close-quarter defense; disarming tactics; and strategy for hostage retrieval.

The Within Arm's Reach method is not a set of techniques from different martial arts or a grab bag of different defensive tactics. Rather, it is a systematic design of principles for all areas of the martial sciences. Part of the curriculum is the integration of principles, concepts and physical applications that can reinforce specific needs for the elite professional of any level. This program does not seek to change the professional; instead, it gives the professional more tools to add to his defensive repertoire.

Most martial artists don't take modern-day weapons use into consideration when they develop their techniques. There needs to be: workable weapons retention techniques for those who legally carry weapons; an understanding of the use of force policies for law enforcement; an ability teach how to protect someone else besides yourself; a method to help someone survive multiple attackers; and easily escalating from a low level of force to deadly force. Gun experts, for the most part, suffer from a reverse problem because their skill is based on the use of deadly force. However, most still lack the same expert skills for lower levels of threats.

Defensive Tactics have great short-term courses with all the preceding elements considered in their planning, but their depth of understanding is limited. Although students may gain a good rudimentary understanding of the technique, they have a hard time expanding or problem-solving within a system. In the martial arts, though, there should be many levels of understanding.

I've integrated the best of both worlds into a quick, dynamic and ever-expanding method that allows you to grow for a long time and be effective in very short time. Close-Quarter Aggressive Defense (C.Q.A.D.) is the basis for all physical intervention skills taught in the Within Arm's Reach method. Firearms use comes under the advanced stages of the weapons' groups. Defending against multiple attackers requires principles and physical skills from W.A.R.'s physical intervention elements.

Here is a basic overview of the Within Arm's Reach physical intervention skill program.

1. The Three-Way Partnership Concept
2. **The Three Stages of Conflict**
3. The Learning of W.A.R.

LEARNING METHODOLOGY
   a. The techniques are easy to learn.
   b. The method is also a basis for the commonality in techniques.
   c. The techniques are always supported by the principles of war (P.O.W).
   d. Each technique is learned by physical and mental rehearsal.
   e. Each technique is also reinforced by learning the threat cues recognition to activate a faster response to a threat.
   f. Using obstructions such as doors, cars, trees, poles and trash bins in your techniques.
   g. The use of common shields, including clipboards, hats, jackets, trashcan tops, curtains, desk drawers, throw rugs and waste paper baskets.
   h. Using environmental weapons, such as chairs, tables, belts, pepper, hot sauce and salsa.
   i. Within Arm's Reach is taught on a number of different levels — basic, intermediate, advanced and continuing advanced. Each technique can be a lesson or course by itself and can be expanded for any level or type of use. Also, the type of student will dictate the level of information, as well as the amount and focus of the different elements of W.A.R.

The Student Types

NON-PROFESSIONAL — A private citizen who is looking for a method to protect himself and his family, because we all assume a position of protection when we walk someone to his car at night; when we agree to take our parents to market because of their age; or when we pick up our children from school, the mall or a friend's house. The non-professional program emphasizes an overview of certain elements such as, awareness techniques, use of force issues, edge of war, impact of war, P.A.C., hostage retrieval, multi-attacks and close-quarter firearms and tactics taught to a dynamic and effective level of combat application in a short time.

THE PROFESSIONAL — Includes security officers, bouncers, police officers, bodyguards and probation officers. Each type of professional would have a program designed for his particular professional need. It's not a one-course-fits-all curriculum. For example, I would give police officers an in-depth look into the elements that focus on controlling a person (PAC). Also, I would stress firearm re-control tactics retention and field of fire control. An officer's personal safety is paramount at all times; unless an officer can protect himself, he will never be able to arrest or protect anyone else.

THE MARTIAL ARTIST — Within Arm's Reach has from the very beginning taught a number of martial arts black belts in various styles and systems how to break down forms and kata. W.A.R. has it own forms, which contain one-and two-man sets to help teach the countless self-defense techniques. These go hand-in-hand with advanced pressure-point applications and the use of angles for striking, throwing and sweeping. This is taught using a platform of lines, which give you reference points to better understand the directions and relationships to your attacker(s).

I learned this from pendekar Paul deThouars, who taught me how to understand forms, pressure points and the way to create a W.A.R. combat platform.

THE ELITE PROFESSIONALS — For members of S.W.A.T., S.S.T., S.E.T., H.R.T., special operations teams and V.I.P. teams. The complete W.A.R. program is taught to every team, however each type of team will have a different mission goal. I design an in-depth program for each type of team to see how the elements of Within Arm's Reach can better identify what areas need to be re-enforced or changed, and what individual and team tactics need to be improved.

I will look at each team in terms of its hand-to-hand, explosive entry, weapons retention, team control of prisoners, or criminals within their use of force guidelines and see how they can be made more efficient and effective. Some Military Special Operations teams, whose training generally is classified, have asked me if I would present my program so they could pick and choose the movements they liked.

Cliff Stewart's S. W.A. T. pin.

Methods of Instruction

Each technique is shown at real speed, then slow speed, and then in sections with detailed explanations of the keys and principles that make the movement 99-percent effective.

1. Lesson format. First we state the types of attacks to be used. They include grabs, locks, chokes, pushes, tackles, takedowns, throws, ground survival, punches, and kicks.

2. If the attacker is armed, what type of weapon is being used — edged weapon, impact or firearm.

3. Which limb is attacking — left, right or both arms or legs.

4. The number of attackers — 1, 2, 3, or 4.

5. Each technique is taught as a progressive use of force within that technique. It begins with a release from grabs or holds, then flows to locks and control, stun or knockout, and finally, deadly force, if justified.

6. The structure of the technique is based on three steps to complete. This is called the base technique.

7. What principles are used in the technique? You only need three or four to be 99-percent successful.

8. Target selection and method of application.

9. Factors used include x, y, or z.

The Formula of W.A.R.

This is a basic breakdown of some of the possible options within the same technique.

1. Base technique plus P.O.W. = specific effect.
2. Base + P.O.W.+ x factor = a change in the specific effect.
3. Base + P.O.W.+ y factor = a change in the specific effect.
4. Base + P.O.W.+ z factor = a change in the specific effect.
5. Base + P.O.W.+ x + y = change.
6. Base + P.O.W.+ y + x = change.
7. Base + P.O.W.+ x + z = change.
8. Base + P.O.W.+ y + z = change.
9. Base + P.O.W.+ x + y + z = change.

This is a basic breakdown of how we expand each technique. They can be expanded, but this is my ideal teaching methodology.

X, Y and Z Factors

X FACTORS
a. Hand strikes, three-quarter fist, palm up, palm down, hammerfist, palm heel, claw, forearm, and open-hand chop.
b. Kicks — Front, chorus line, stomping, low sidekick, cut kick, and backkick.
c. Compressions to the neck, face and head.
d. Locks.

Y FACTORS
a. Takedowns — Cross-body, single leg, double leg, arm wrap and drag drop.
b. Throws — Side, shoulder, body, and head.

Z FACTOR
Weapons
a. Impact, edged and firearms.

P.O.W. of W.A.R.

Breaking the Vertical Plane. This is accomplished by moving a person's head past his hips. We are bipeds (we stand vertically). Our head, shoulders, hips and legs stay in a natural alignment. Any changes in this basic structure will weaken a person's ability to fight back. You break the vertical plane by pulling and compressing the head backward and forward.

Attacking Their Alignment. I bis is accomplished by pushing the shoulders and hips at different angles.

Attacking the Base (Legs). Spreading, lifting, buckling, compressing, striking, restricting movement, breaking and dislocating and sweeping the foot or feet accomplish this.

Displacement of Balance. This is accomplished when a person takes a step, puts his weight on the heels or puts his weight on the balls of his feet.

Understanding and Using Angles. This will assist you in taking the balance away from a person when striking, throwing and locking. For weapon usage and weapon retention, the angles that will make the difference between success and failure are 45 degrees, 90 degrees, 30 degrees and 15 degrees.

Target Selection and Methods of Application. Understanding the locations, spots, places and methods that will weaken a persons basic areas of attack. These are the nerves, tendons, organs and ligaments. Combining these formulas weakens the body.

The symbols of W.A.R. This is a method of applying pressure points to symbols, with each symbol representing locations or points on the body. I use an ax, tree, water bucket, burning logs, earth and a light switch as switches. When these symbols are combined, the degree of success will range from possible-to-highly probable and can cause pain, numbness, unconsciousness, permanent damage or even death. Each symbol can destroy another symbol and when properly combined will cause a great deal of damage to the attacker.

    a. The ax can cut the tree
    b. The tree can stick into the ground.
    c. The earth will absorb the bucket of water.
    d. The fire will melt the ax and burn the tree.
    e. The water will extinguish the flame.

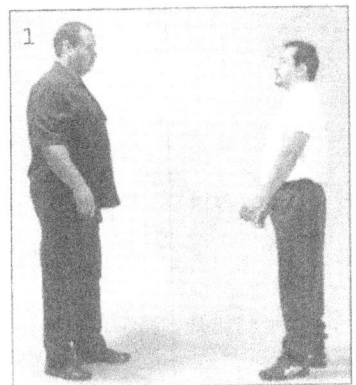

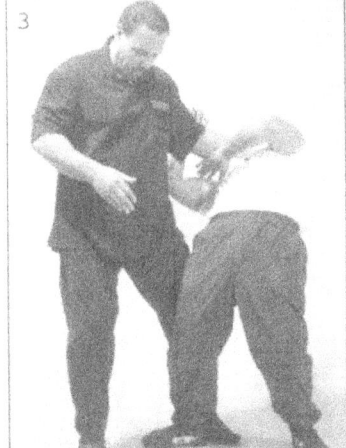

BREAKING THE VERTICAL PLANE. From an on-guard (1), move in and push his head back (2) to break the vertical plane (3).

Compression

Lifting

Striking

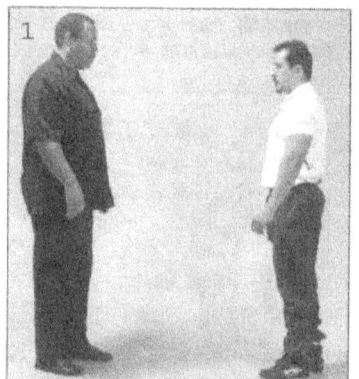

Start (1). Attack the shoulder alignment (2-3).

Attacking the hip. From an on-guard position (1), attack the hip alignment to create a fold (2). This will be the result (3).

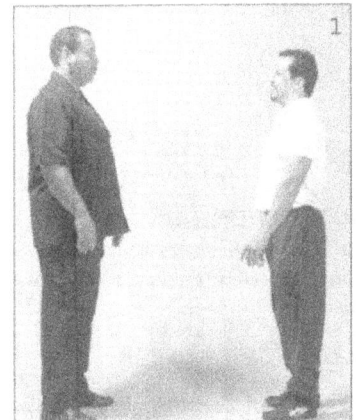

From on-guard position (1), move and strike at a 45-degree angle (2-3) to take his balance (4).

Limb Associated Points (L.A.P.)

This method shows you a way to weaken the body by using the concept of Body Mirror Imaging or L.A.P. You can learn dozens of pressure points in a matter of hours. Once you understand the concepts and principles you can weaken the legs, arms and head, control holds, and apply jointlocks, takedowns, and sweeps.

TRANSFERING ENERGY INTO YOUR STRIKES, THROWS AND LOCKS
   a. Half-Squat
   b. Step Forward Stance
   c. Step Backward Stance
   d. Tactical Positioning: Placing yourself in a position of power and advantage
   e. Aggressive Defense: Attacking the attacker, intercepting and destroying the attack itself

LINES OF RESISTANCE AND REACTION
This requires an understanding of how humans react when struck or how they will react when you're trying to place them under control. By understanding the possible ways they will resist, you will know how to counter.

INDEXING
Indexing is punching any hand weapon (empty or full, firearm, knife or impact weapon) into the attacking limb and/or person.

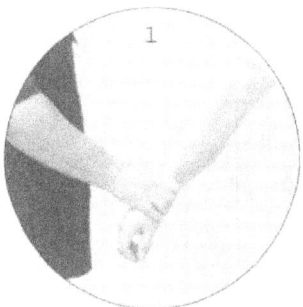

The light switch. This involves a series of nerves located around the wrist. By torquing it, you can create a weakness in the wrist and hand.

Fire 11. Roll the knuckles and punch down on the triceps tendon.

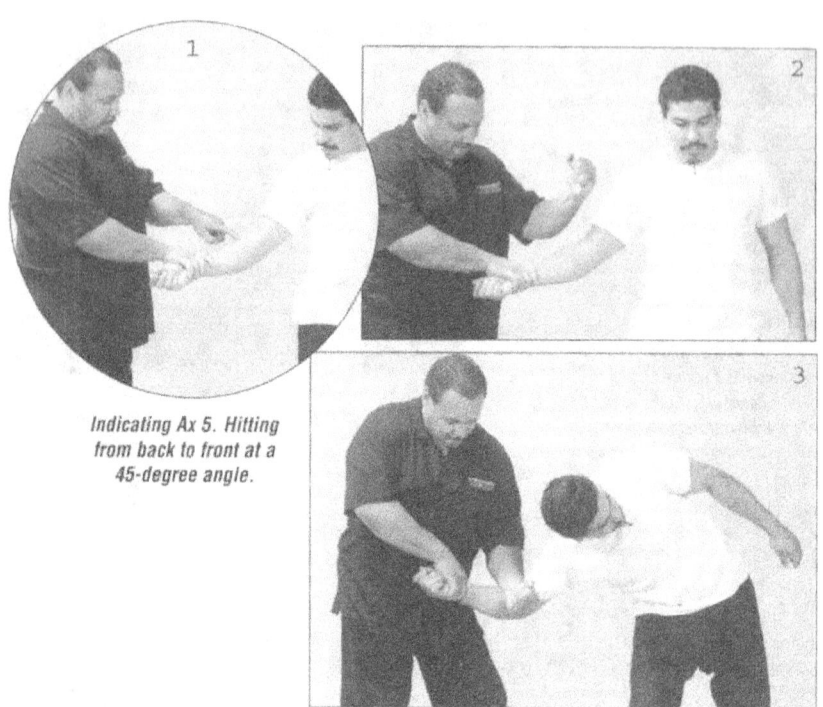

Indicating Ax 5. Hitting from back to front at a 45-degree angle.

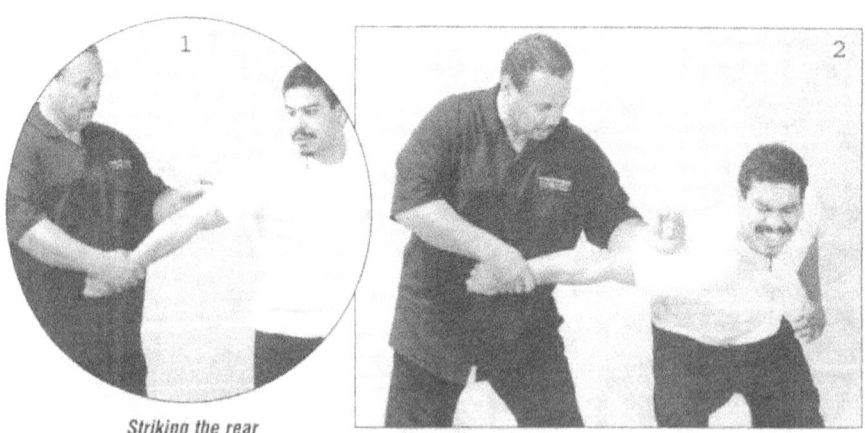

Striking the rear deltoid at 45 degrees.

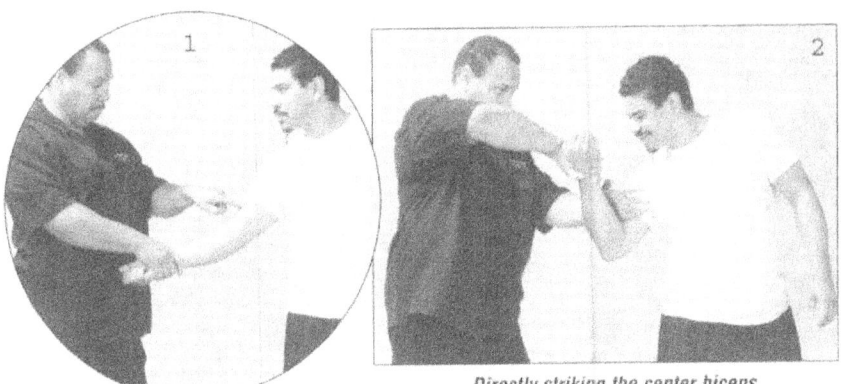

Directly striking the center biceps can cause the arm to go numb.

Punching the biceps in the center. This can be dangerous because it can effect the heart.

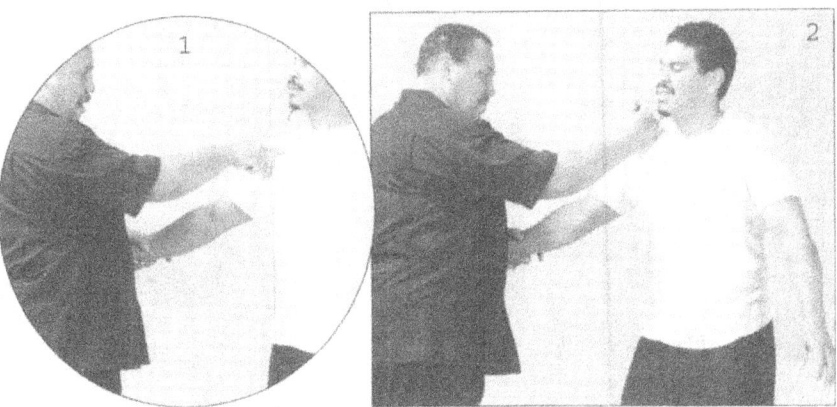

Earth 15. Hammerstrike down to the muscle just below the clavicle. This releases the legs and also seals the lungs.

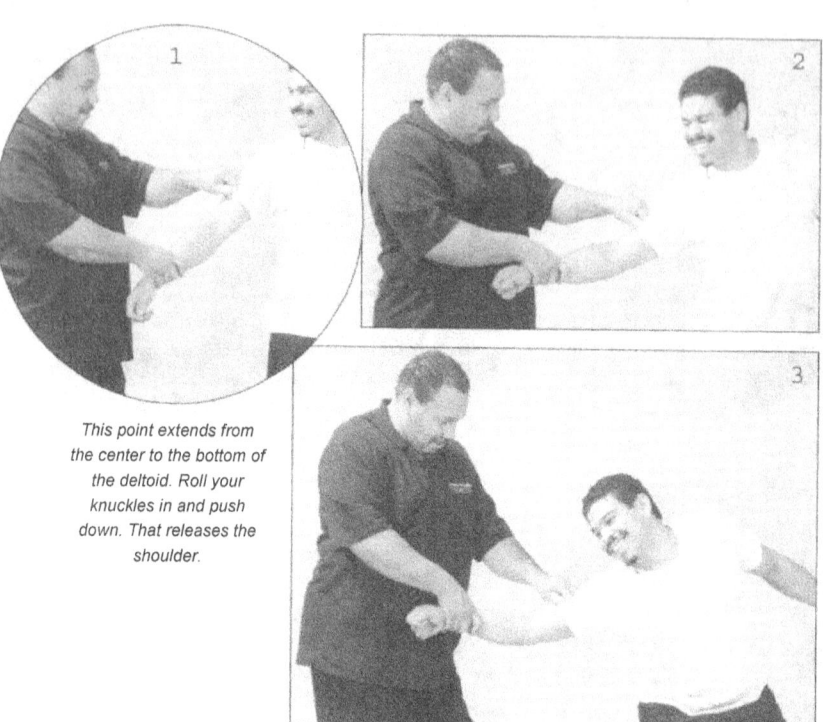

This point extends from the center to the bottom of the deltoid. Roll your knuckles in and push down. That releases the shoulder.

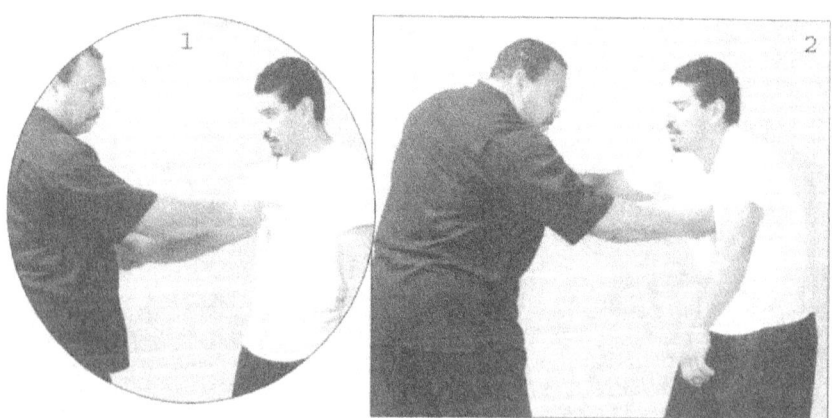

A straight shot to the center sternum with the knuckle.

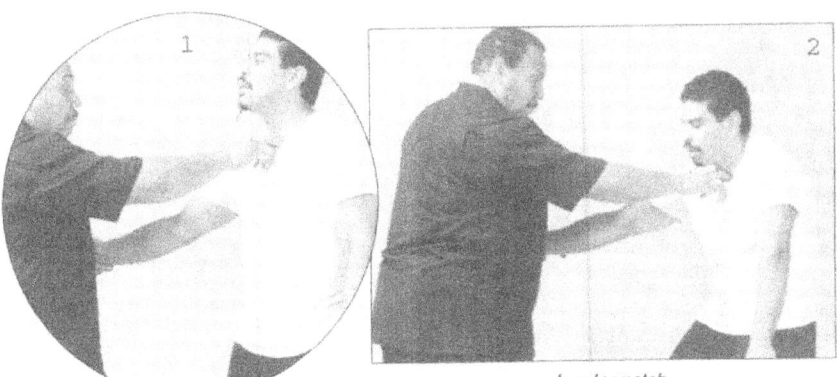
Jugular notch.

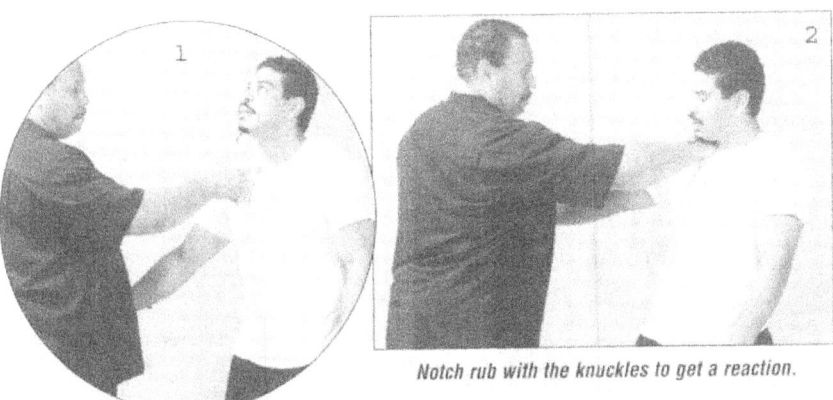
Notch rub with the knuckles to get a reaction.

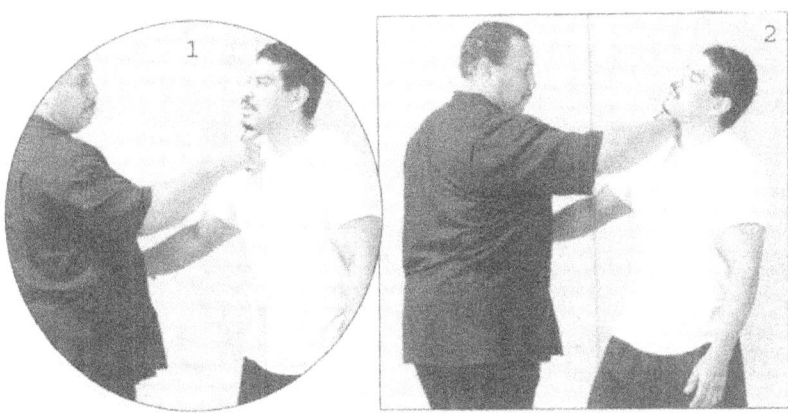
Ax 18. This is a 45-degree strike from the back to the side of the neck, which can cause unconsciousness.

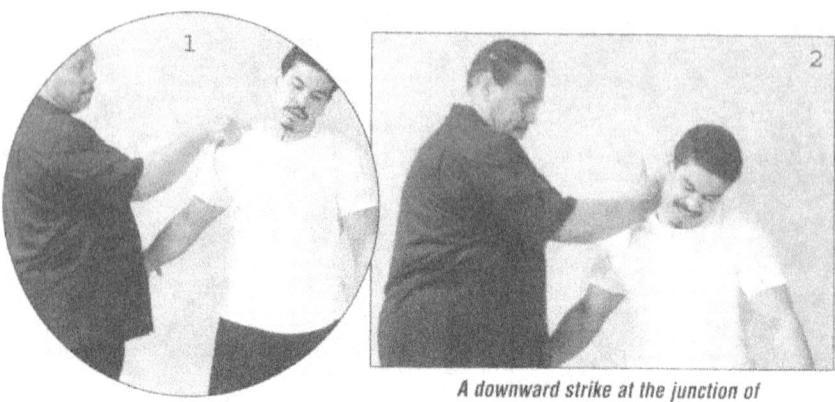

A downward strike at the junction of the trapezius and the neck.

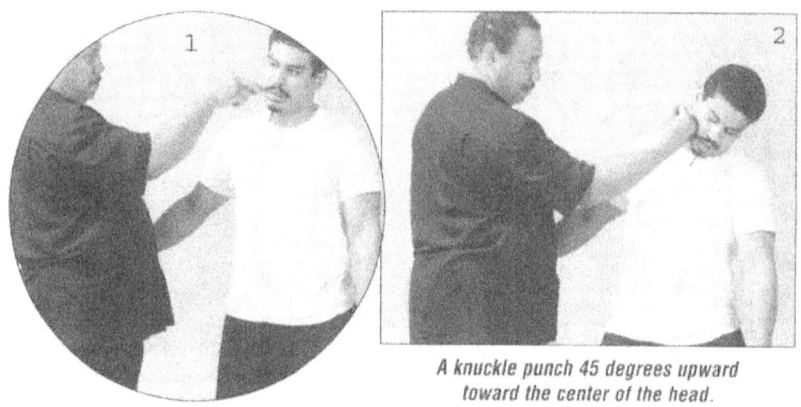

A knuckle punch 45 degrees upward toward the center of the head.

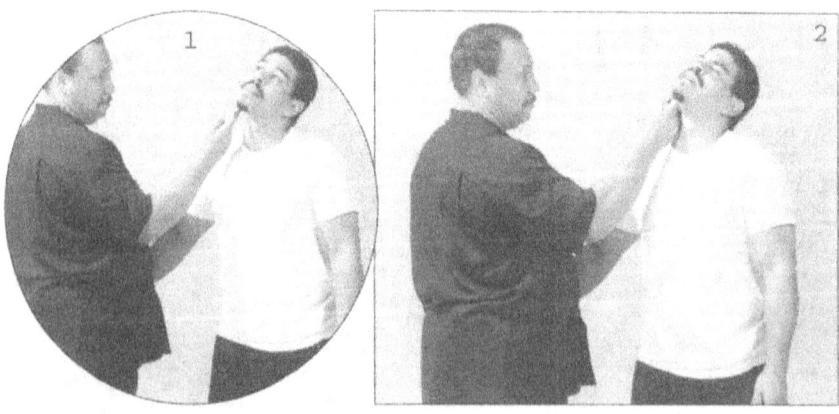

Earth 5. Under the jaw. Knuckle punch straight up. This also can cause unconsciousness.

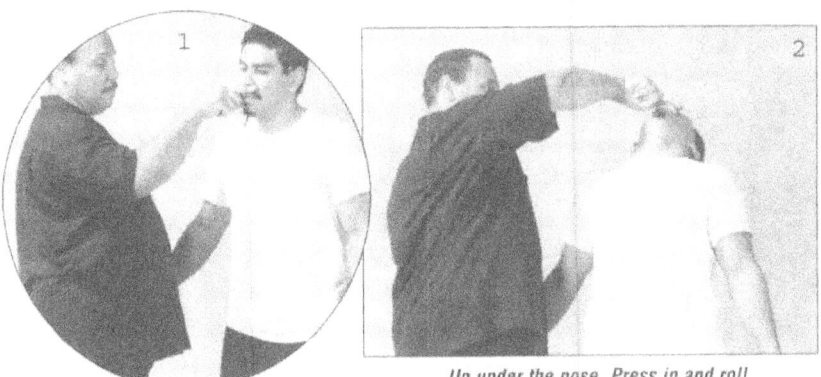

Up under the nose. Press in and roll up to help break the vertical plane.

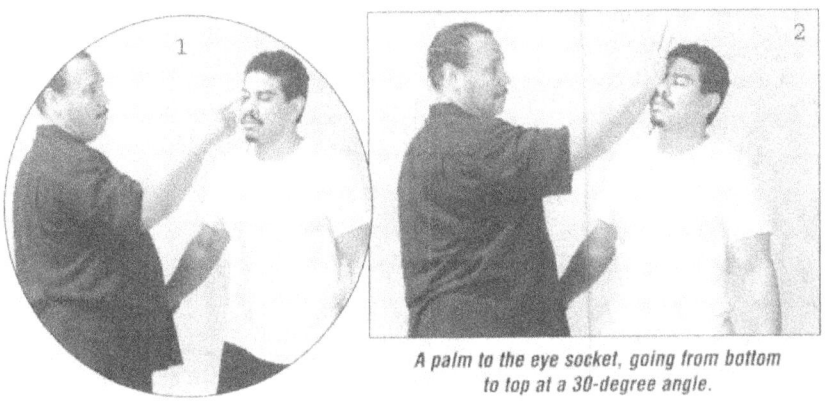

A palm to the eye socket, going from bottom to top at a 30-degree angle.

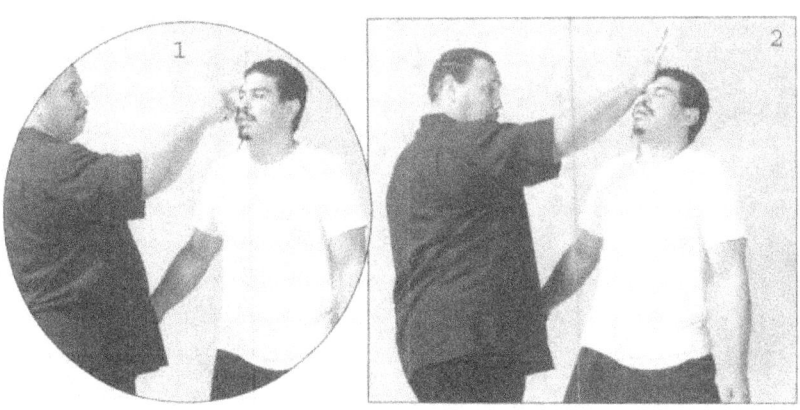

A strike to the center third eye. This strike either goes up or down.

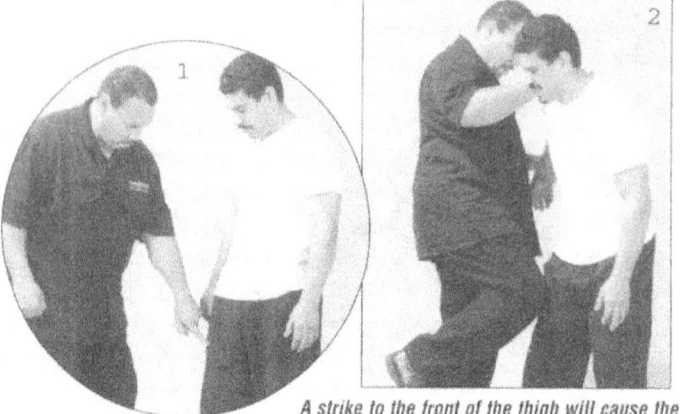

A strike to the front of the thigh will cause the leg to hyperextend and lead to weakness in the arm and leg.

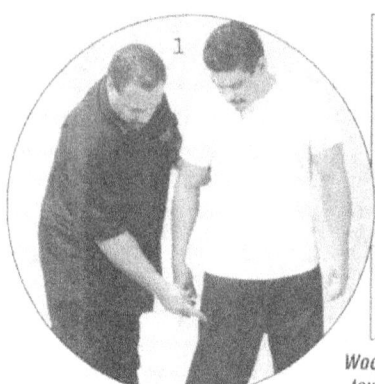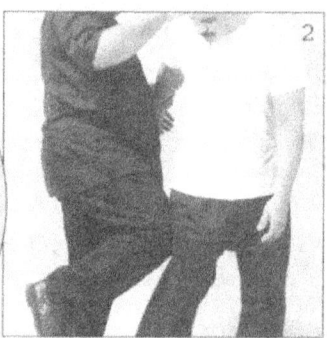

Wood 31. Can be found at the side of the thigh, located toward the end of your fingertips if you stand straight.

Inner gate. A kick will set up head points.

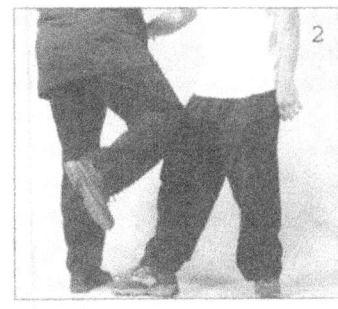

Wood 9. The inside of the thigh in the middle. Striking this point can cause the leg to turn out and collapse.

Earth 10. This point can be found above the knee. Struck at a 45-degree angle, it will cause the leg to buckle.

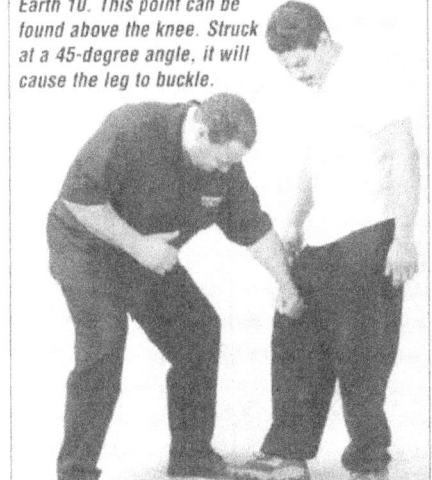

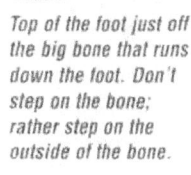

Top of the foot just off the big bone that runs down the foot. Don't step on the bone; rather step on the outside of the bone.

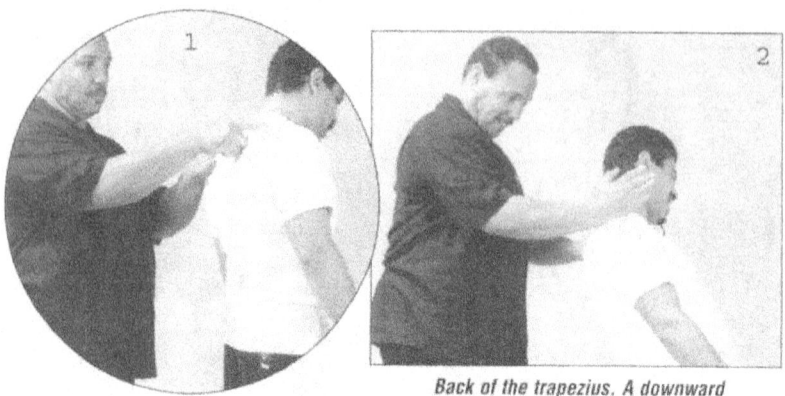

Back of the trapezius. A downward
strike will weaken your legs.

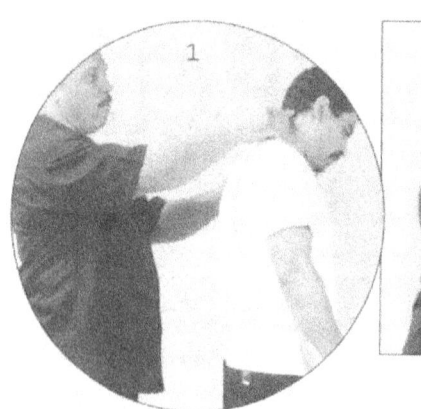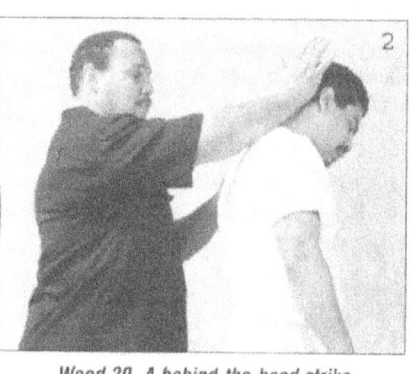

Wood 20. A behind-the-head strike
with the upper palm.

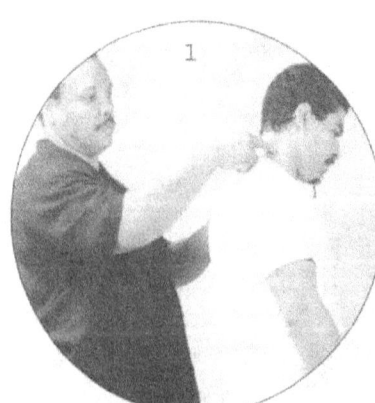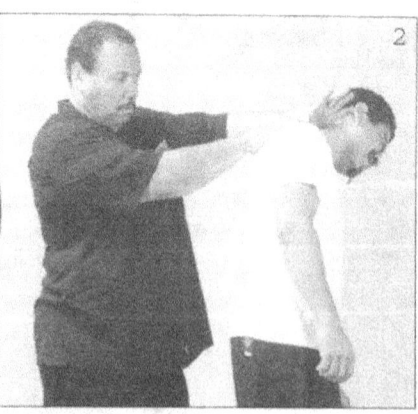

Opposite of Ax 18. Striking the rear side of the
neck from back to front.

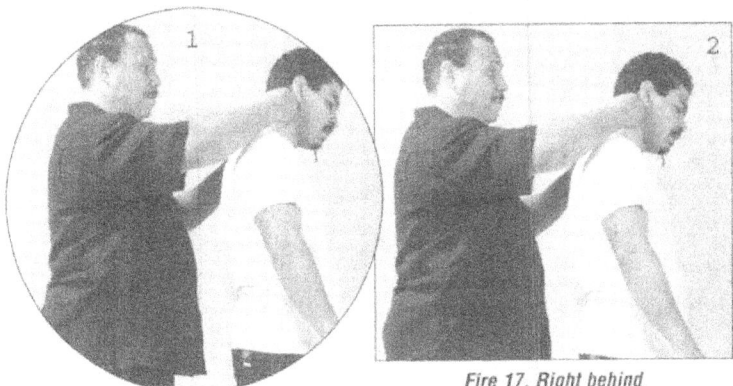

Fire 17. Right behind the back of your ear.

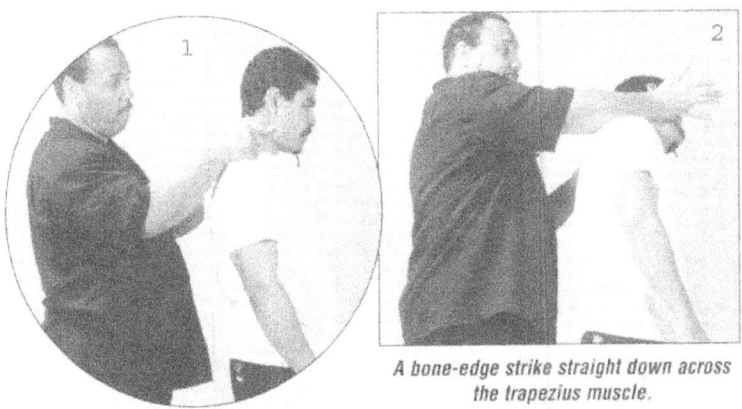

A bone-edge strike straight down across the trapezius muscle.

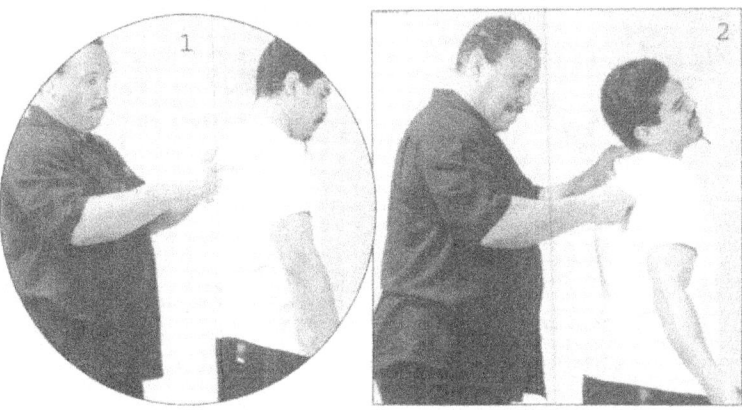

Striking to the soft, cushy area of the should blade.

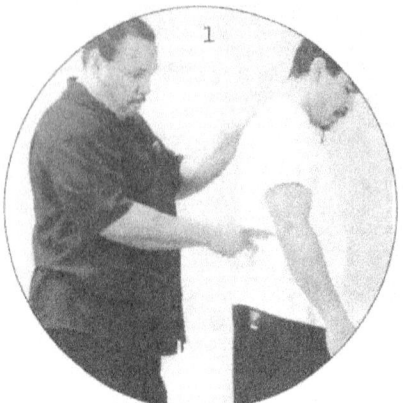 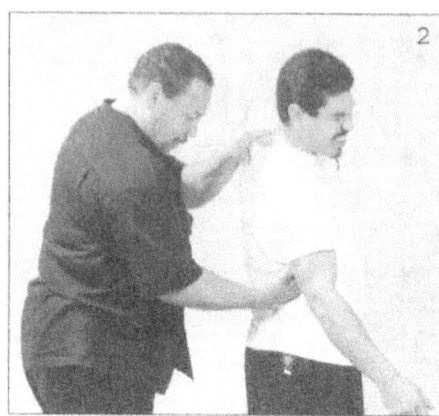

Kidney strike. Where the elbow falls when arms are hung to the sides. Most people, however, strike too low.

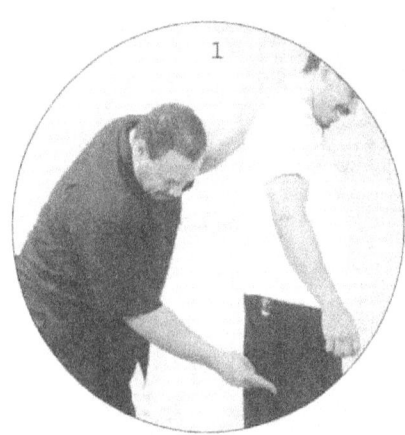 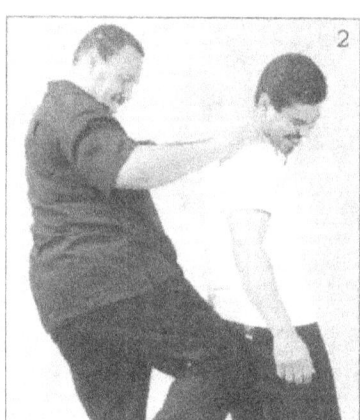

Leg biceps center.

Achilles' tendon ankle.

High calf.

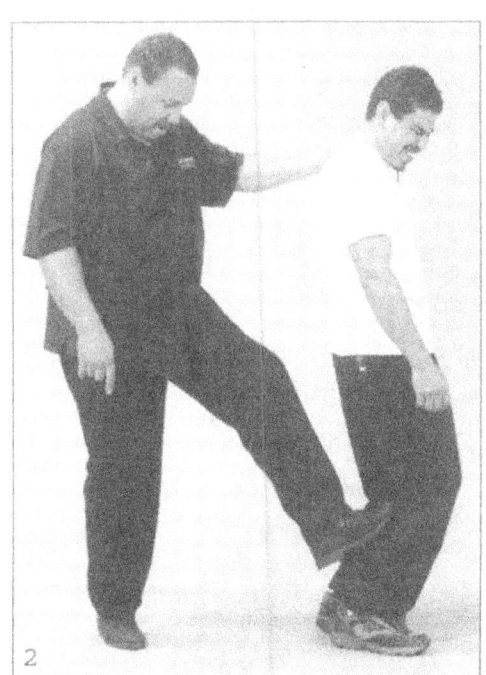

Hostage Retrieval

FIELD OF CONTROL — The area where you limit your tactics while protecting someone else.

The Breath of W.A.R.
a. Beep (speed)
b. Exhale (deep or quick)
c. Inhale (pulling or lifting)

Within Arm's Reach Self-Defense Tactics
a. The three levels of application
b. Reverse motion
c. Front-to-back/Back-to-front
d. Inside/Outside
e. Tools can be exchanged

The Warm-Up
The W.A.R. warm-up has a two-fold purpose: physical conditioning and developing the body's tools for combat.

	Workout	Combat
		Butting

1. Head Flexing
   a. Forward
   b. Backward.
   c. Sideways
	Neck	

2. Shoulder Rotations Shoulders	Bumping	Lifting

3. Elbows
   Shoulders/Back
   a. Across
   b. Flapping
   c. Vertical
   d. Backward
   e. Circular
   f. Downward
		Elbow
		Striking

4. Legs
   a. Four corners Quads/leg biceps Buckling
   b. Leg flap
   c. Four corners and slide
   d. Chorus line front, side, oblique Kicking
		Spreading Sweeping

5. Stomach — Legendary Abs

6. **Ladder Push-Ups** — 5 Positions Down and Up with a 10-second hold on each position

7. HFL Power Stretching

8. **Touch a Point** — Touching your body where pressure points are located. Learning proper angles and directions.

THE MAJOR PHYSICAL INTERVENTION ELEMENTS ASSOCIATED WITH WITHIN ARM'S REACH:

A. Close-quarter aggressive defense
    b. Protective assault control
    c. Edge of war
    d. Impact of war
    e. Hostage retrieval
    f. Multi-assault
    g. Close-quarter aggressive firearms

Close-Quarter Aggressive Defense (C.Q.A.D.) provides the foundation for developing techniques against punches, kicks, tackles, throws, and grabs. It also helps with ground survival and builds the basic physical skills for the remaining elements of war. The core of my personal defense method is the progressive aggressive lift method®. We call it the 14- count because of the number of movements in the drill. Some martial artists might say it resembles something seen in various disciplines, such as Filipino kali hubut lubut, Japan's mawasi uke, Indonesian silat, wing chun, or tai chi chuan. And you would be right, because all those elements and principles are enclosed in this multi-level drill.

There are ten different levels of understanding to this drill. It develops coordination, speed, proper tool usage, and improved reaction time. It can be learned in a few hours and the retention rate is very high. Most of my students can remember the 14-count years later after just a 20-minute refresher.

This is the core protection and entry system for W.A.R. We do not wait for the attack to be completed, nor do we take on a passive cover-up defensive position. We meet the attack while it's in progress or prepare to grab and strike. We will intercept the attack by attacking the attacker, attacking the limb or both. This will help reduce your reaction time. Each motion is actually a nerve strike with the palm or bone edge of your arm. With a turn of the hand you can attack the eyes or grab the wrist in one simple but sophisticated movement.

The lower body aids in the aggressive attitude by applying knees or kicks. As we enter and step down we attack the attacker's base with a multitude of options, including sweeping, buckling, compressing or lifting. There is a saying in W.A.R class: "Every time we touch you we cause pain or injury." This necessitates the fine-tuning of such anatomical weapons as the heel palm, knifehand, vertical fist, hammerfist, elbows and low-line kicks. These are practiced as tool sets by emphasizing non-telegraphic delivery from a relaxed (non-preparatory stance) position.

The Basic Progressive Aggressive Lift Series (R.A.L. 14-count level one)

HERE ARE A FEW EXAMPLES OF THE EXPANDING LEVELS OF P.A.L.

    A.   Parry circle grab or strike
    B.   Parry bone edge
    C.   Parry circle across
    D.   Lift parry trap strike
    E.   You can reverse the order of the motions
    E X, Y and Z options

THE 14-COUNT

#	Motion	Strike Target
1.	Parry lift outside straight right.	To the face
2.	Parry lift outside straight left.	To the face
3.	Parry lift inside straight left.	To the face
4.	Parry lift inside straight right.	To the face
5.	Drop down left, straight right.	To the solar plexus
6.	Drop down right, straight left.	To the solar plexus
7.	Reverse palm, stop for wide right hook.	To the face
8.	Reverse palm, stop for wide left hook.	To the face
9.	P.A.L. for a low right body hook.	To the body
10.	P.A.L. for low left body hook.	To the body
11.	P.A.L. pass for low right hook.	To the body
12.	P.A.L. pass for low left hook.	To the body
13.	P.A.L. low wedge for two-hand low grab.	To the body
14.	P.A.L. high wedge for two-hand high grab.	To the body

TYPICAL FREE-FLOWING EXERCISE

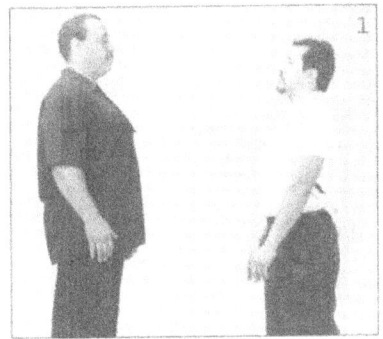
Start.

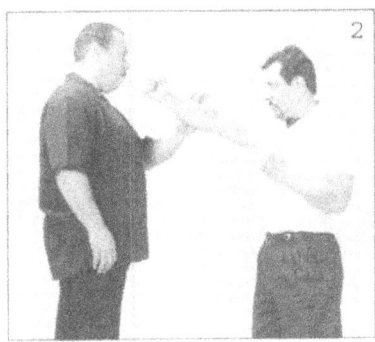
Parry left hand against right punch.

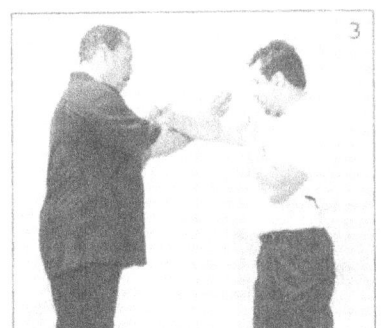
Right arm lifts under punch.

Left punch to the face, right parry.

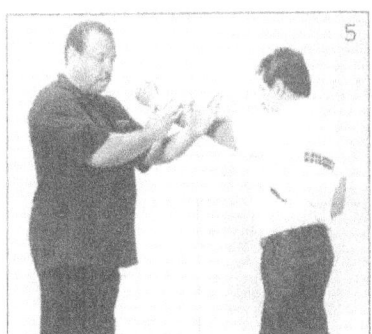
Left lift.

Right punch to the face, right inside parry.

TYPICAL FREE-FLOWING EXERCISE continued

Left lift.

Left punch to the face, left parry.

Right lift.

Right wide hook to the face. Left palm facing check.

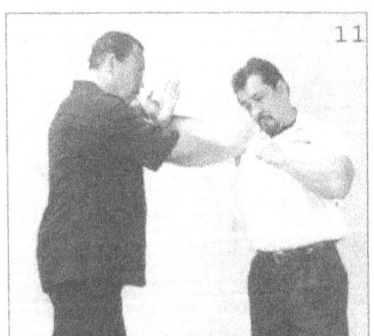

Palm down to shoulder.

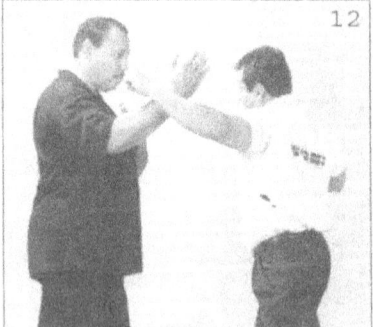

Right palm to shoulder.

TYPICAL FREE-FLOWING EXERCISE *continued*

Right punch to the stomach, left dropping palm.

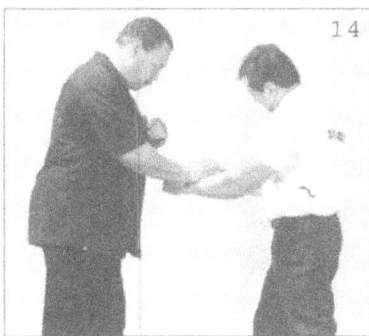

Left punch to the stomach, right dropping palm.

Left wide hook to the face. Right palm facing check.

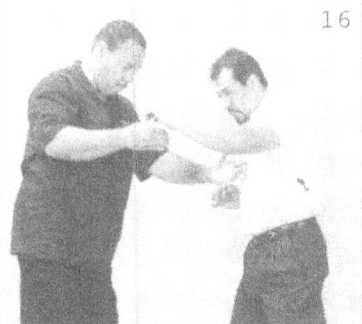

Left palm to shoulder.

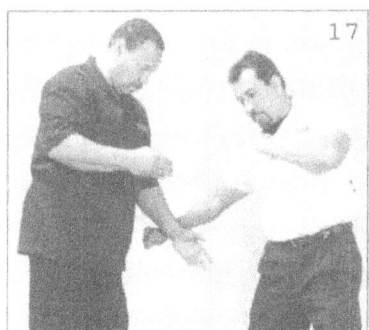

Low right hook to the body,

Left drop.

TYPICAL FREE-FLOWING EXERCISE *continued*

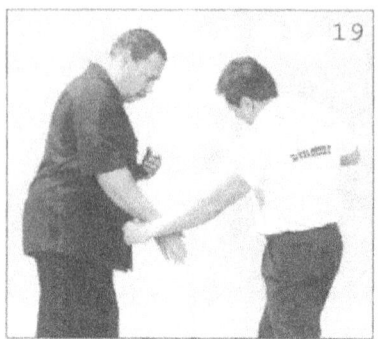
Right palm to inside biceps lift.

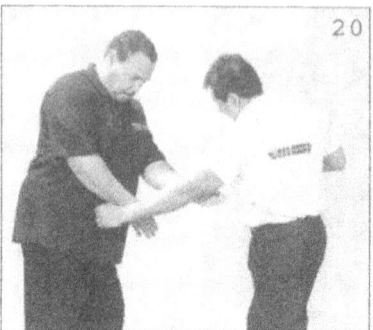
Low left hook to the body, right hand drop.

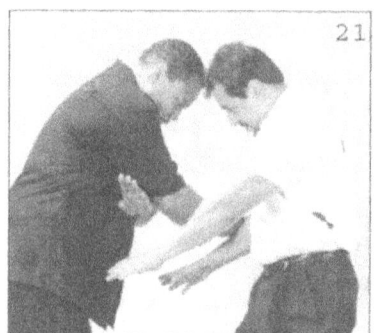
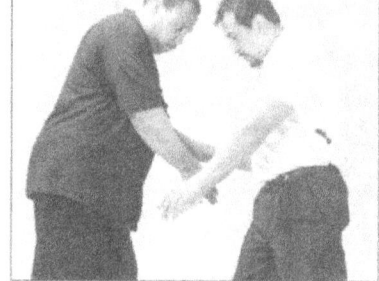
Left lifting palm to the biceps.

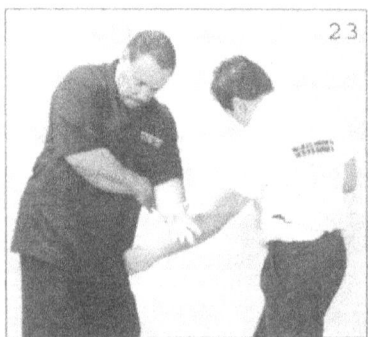
Right low hook to the body pass.

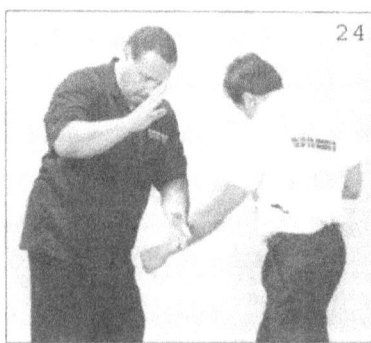
Low left hook to the body.

TYPICAL FREE-FLOWING EXERCISE *continued*

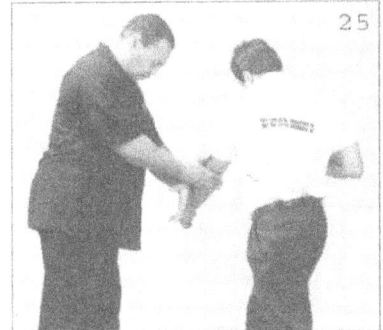

Circular palm cup to elbow to control.

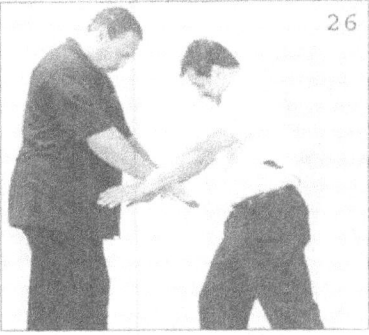

Two-hand low grab. The counter is a double-hand wedge.

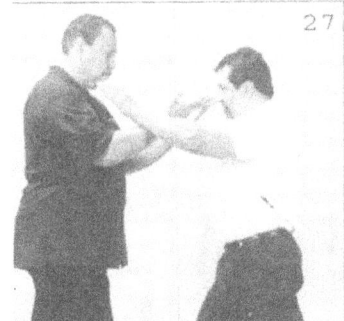

From low hand, do a two-hand choke high.

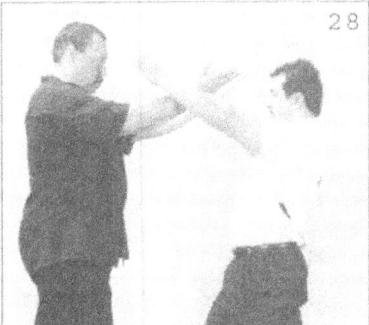

p_ng the sequence with a two-hand palm-up wedge.

14-COUNT APPLICATIONS

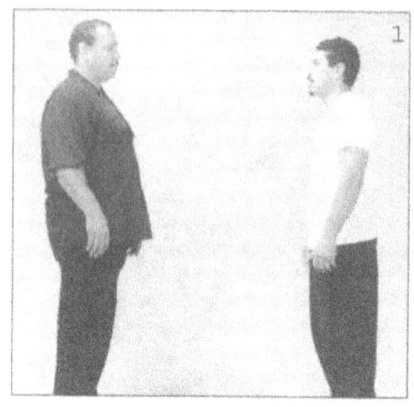

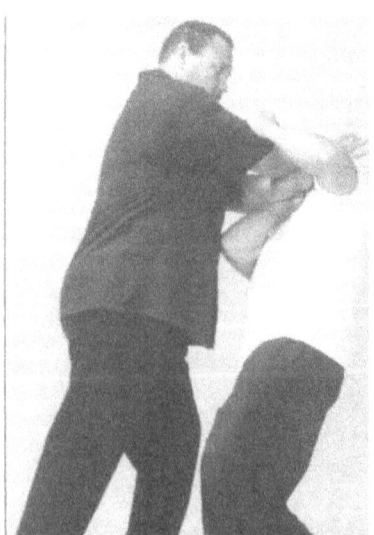

APPLICATION OF THE 14-COUNT
This is part of the teaching methodology of the escalation of force.

KNOCKOUT
Start (1). As the attacker high hooks to the head, left parry strike (2) to Ax 5. Right chop to low biceps as the left hand chops to the side of the neck (3). Twist counterclockwise as you strike (4). Follow up with an elbow to the chin (5).

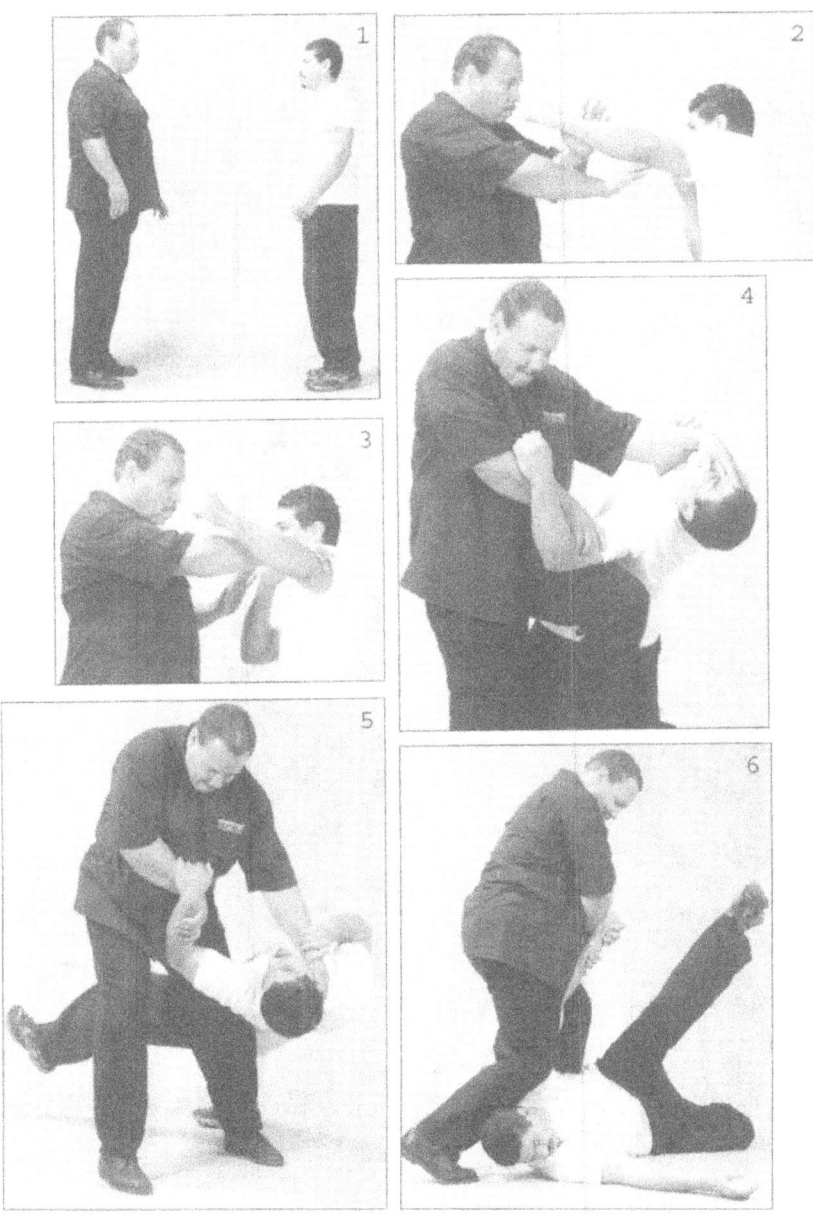

TAKEDOWN

Start (1). The attacker opens with a left high hook to the face (2). Parry, chop and grab the left wrist (3). Step forward as your left hand palms to the face (4). Bump the hip as you move into a horse stance, keeping pressure on as you break his plane (5). Horse stance as he drops to the ground. Pull on his arm and drop your knee on his shoulder, face or neck (6).

14-COUNT APPLICATIONS

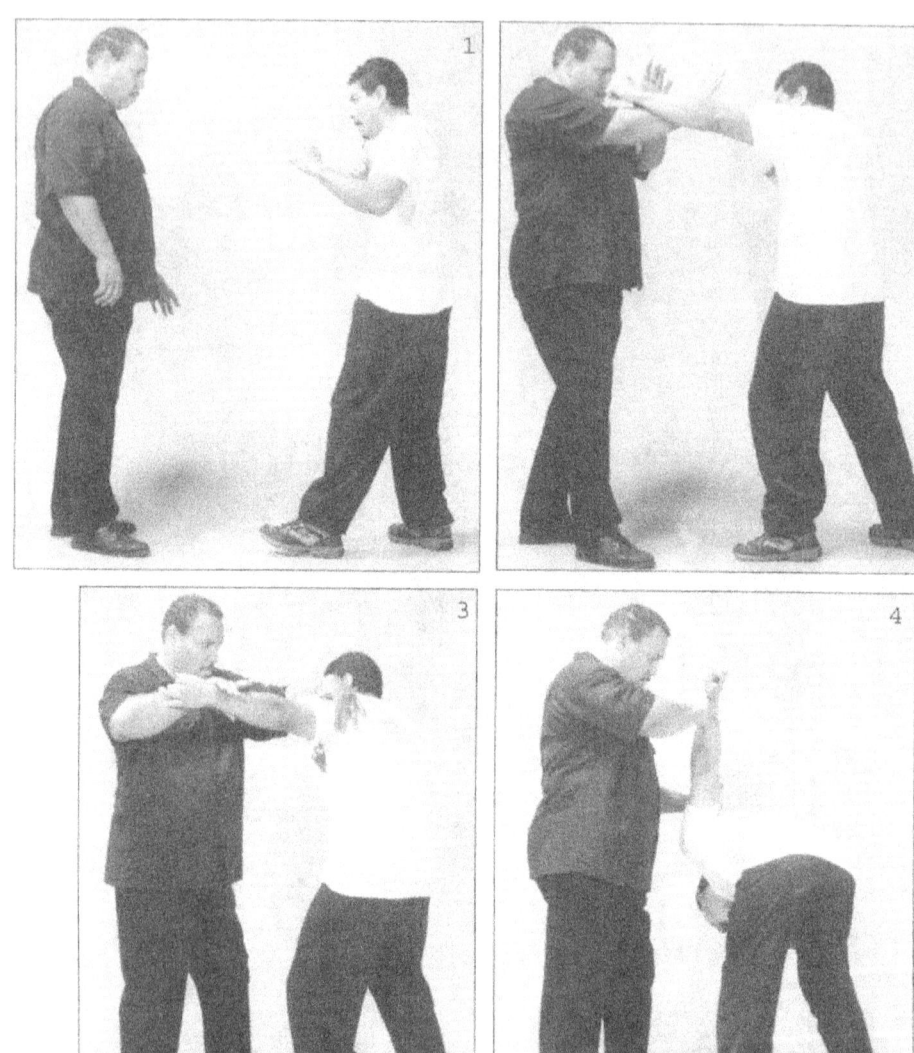

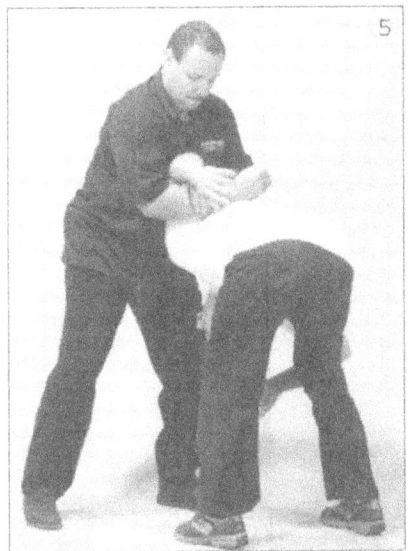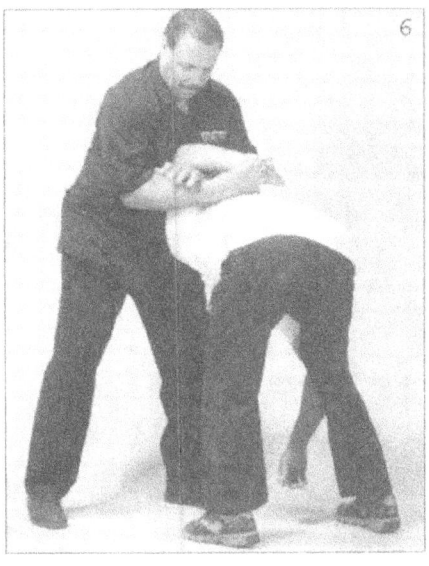

LOCK

From the on-guard (1), a high left hook to the face is met with a parry and chop (2). Your right hand grabs his wrist and left hand pulls on the rear of his shoulder (3). The right hand pushes and left hand pulls, which drops him forward (4). Apply a hammerlock as you hip bump the side of your opponent's neck to unbalance him (5). Keep knee hip pressure on the side of his neck as you rotate your lock to your left (6). Maintain pressure on his neck with your hip as you rotate the lock to your left. Now lift (7).

14-COUNT APPLICATIONS

LOW HOOK
Start (1). A low left hook is met with a chop to the side of the neck (2). Knee to wood pile for the knockout (3).

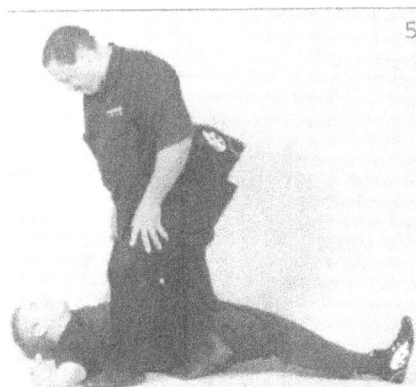

TAKEDOWN

The opponent fires a low left hook to the body (1). Block the the low hook to the body by wedging and palming to the rear of the left ear (2). Wrap under his arm as you step forward to the outside of his right leg with your right leg (3). Turn counter-clockwise to drop him (4). Knee drop to his groin (5).

14-COUNT APPLICATIONS

LOCK

Start (1). Move into a wedge (2). The left hand goes behind his head, pulling him forward (3). Reverse shoulder brace (4), then compress and kneel down to control (5).

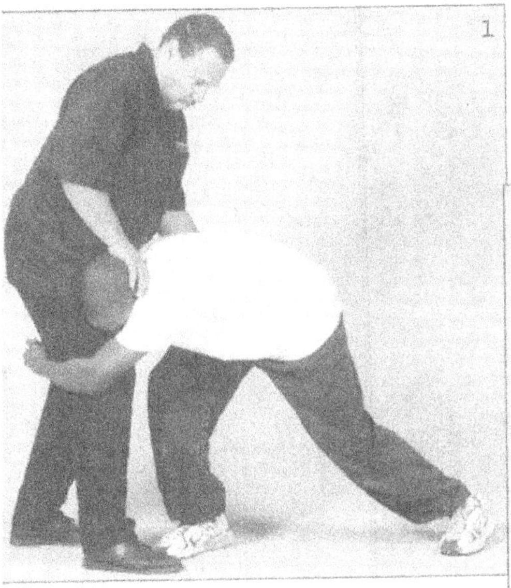

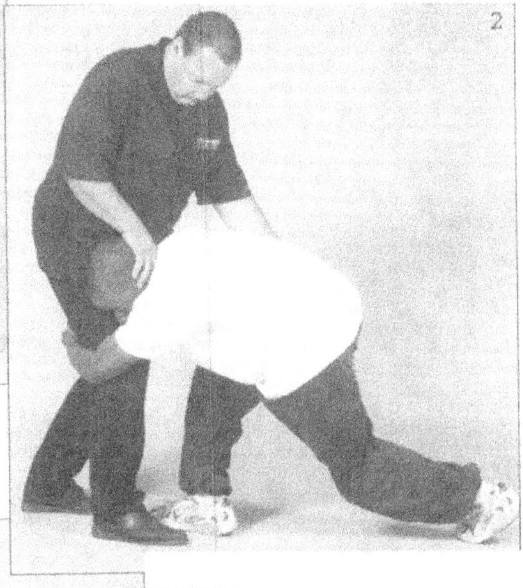

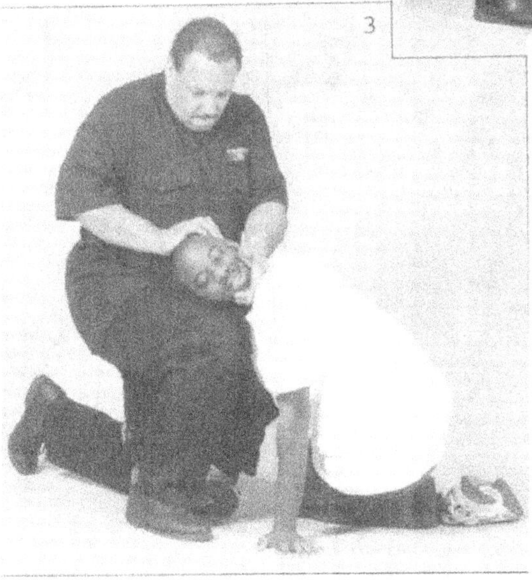

TACKLE

As the grab occurs, I turn my right foot 45 degrees outward (1). Push his hips and head down (2). Drop to one knee and push his head down (3). Put pressure on his head for a neck crank.

14-COUNT APPLICATIONS

MID-LEVEL FRONT KICK
Start (1). From a front kick to the groin, start body rotation with your left hand down (2). Rotate to the right and strike on the inside inner gate (3). As his foot lands and your shoulder is pointing toward his landing foot, kick to the knee (4).

REAR CHOKE

Start in a rear choke position (1). As he bends back, turn clockwise with your shoulder and hips (2). Drop the chin and push on his hip (3). Continue to turn and push on his shoulder. Step between his legs and do a one-eighth squat. As he falls, pinch him in the armpit (4).

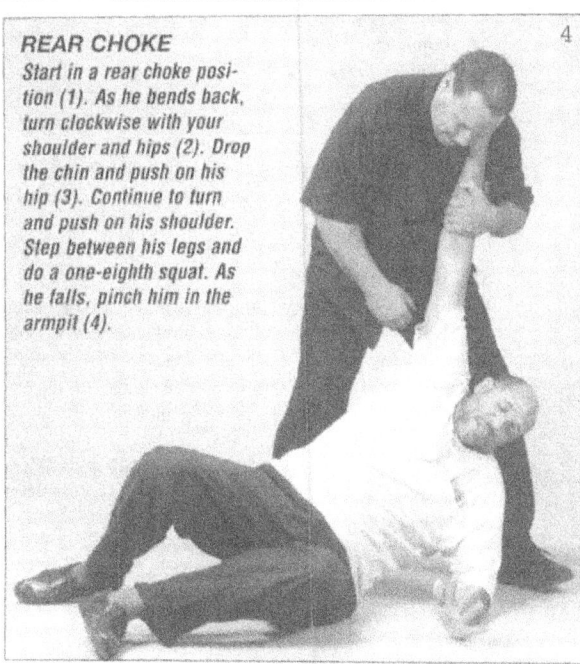

Protective Assault Control (P.A.C.)

Protective Assault Control (P.A.C.) is what I teach in the Within Arm's Reach program to control or lock a person. The program consists of the five major principles that will help you perform every type of lock or control and give you an understanding of the differences between locking and controlling. I teach the five primary locks, as well as face and neck compression. I also teach use-of-force laws, ground survival and pressure point strikes, and foul tactics.

These are the five major principles that will allow you to perform any type of lock.

1. Hyperextending the limb — Straighten it past its natural range of motion.
2. **Twisting** — A limb, hand or foot until it locks and then take it beyond the lock position to sprain, dislocate or break.
3. Bending — A limb, foot, wrist or neck until it is frozen. Anytime you pass a locked position you will cause some type of injury. The degree and amount of injury will depend on the energy you put into the lock.
4. **Compression** — Pressure placed against the joints and neck by squeezing or pushing the joints together.
5. **Combinations** — Combining the preceding principles to compound and overload the point of attack for any locks.

The five primary locks taught in P.A.C. are:

1. **Straight arm bar**
2. **Hammerlock**
3. **Shoulder brace**
4. **Figure-four**
5. **Gooseneck**

There are three additional locks taught for every primary lock, plus counters for each primary lock. Also taught are ground survival tactics and how you can adapt the principles of WAR. to P.A.C.

STRAIGHT ARM BAR
When applying the straight arm bar, first pay close attention to the hand of the controlled person. Next, the little finger of the controlled person's should also be up. Understand the points on the arm that you're going to attack and know how striking them will affect other parts of the body. The first point is three fingers above the elbow. By rubbing or pressing, it will straighten the arm and release the shoulder to put a person down. The next point is the center triceps, which is a hit point that will lock the elbow. You can then drop your knees to the ground and cause a heavy stun. You can break the arm by rubbing and hitting the triceps points in combination.

HAMMERLOCK

When using the hammerlock, pay close attention to the elbow. Use the concept of compounding when possible. One way is to push the elbow down and lift the wrist. This places a great deal of pressure on the rotator cuff and the elbow joint. Again, the Within Arm's Reach method can help you expand your understanding of how to be more effective without adding new techniques.

Shoulder Brace Key Points: This technique is most often used when the person being hammerlocked tries to straighten his arm. The basic key points are elbow rotation, angles and footwork.

The Figure-4 Key Points: Elbow placement, body angle, footwork, and pressure points.

The Gooseneck Key Points: The wrist is compressed against your body, which acts as the brace. You attack the hip alignment by bumping or pushing to unbalance the attacker.

STRAIGHT ARM BAR

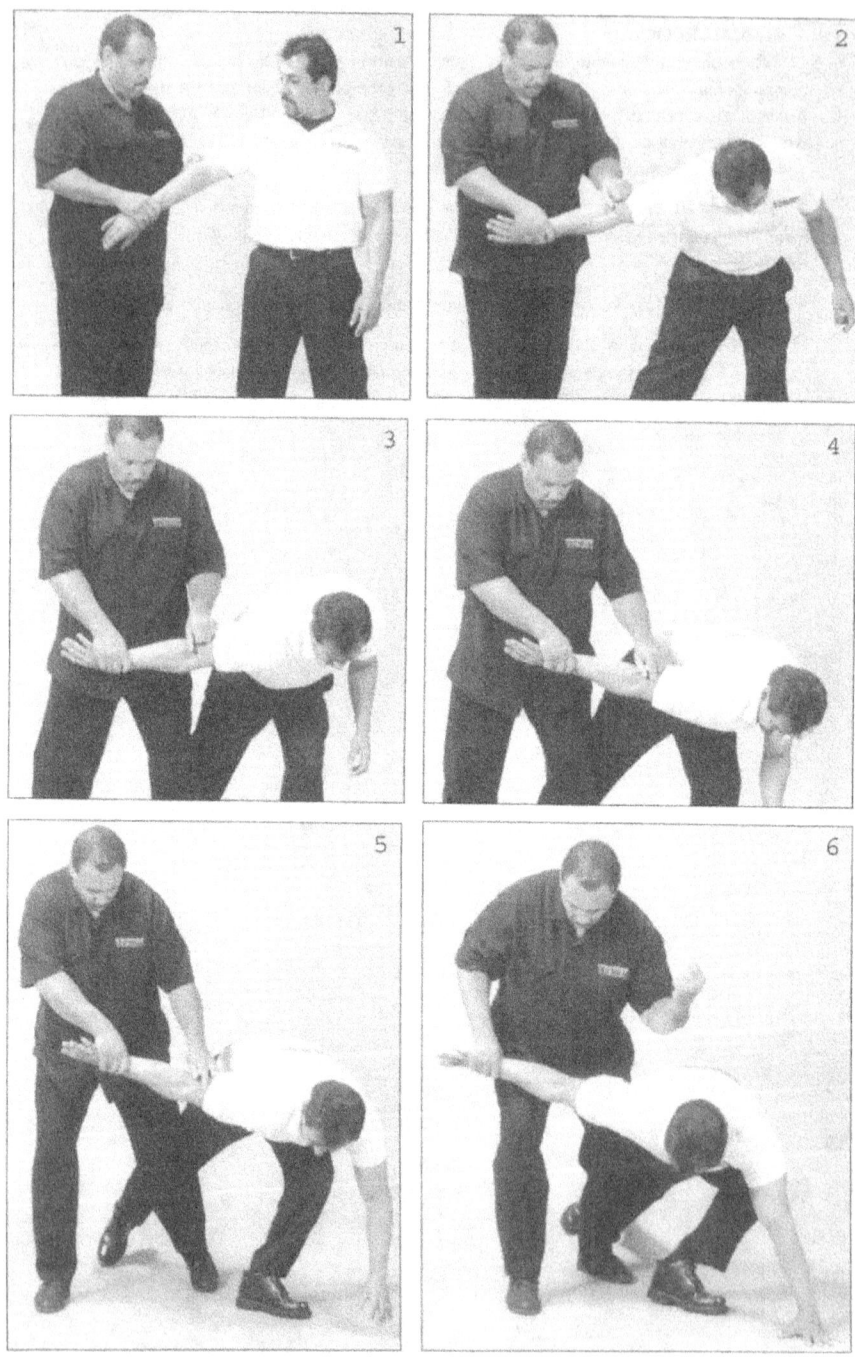

Grabbing the light switch. Use the web hand to grab behind the elbow (1). Twist the light switch and then push on Fire 11. Now push him down (2). Foot step to the front (3). Push across to unbalance the shoulders (4). To maintain control, step forward, pushing at a 45-degree angle on the arm to maintain control (5). Strike to Wood 20 if needed (6).

But if your foot is behind instead of in front, push the top of his shoulders forward and your rear foot attacks his calf. Maintain pressure on the arm (7). If you find your foot on the side instead of the rear, push his arm to your left, turn and drop your right knee to his shin (8). Keep pressure on his arm and shoulders. Compress the arm to maintain control.

FIGURE-FOUR

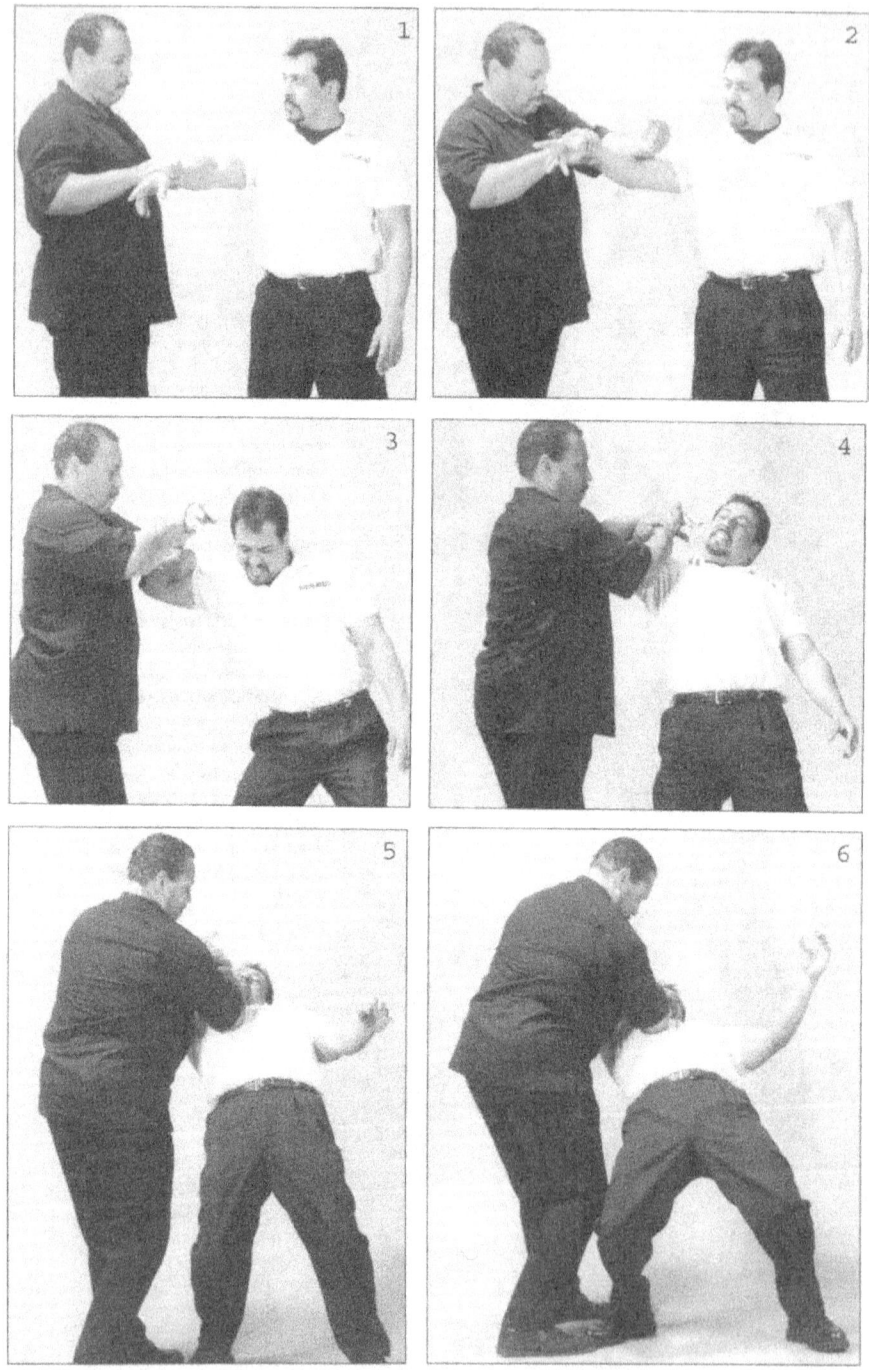

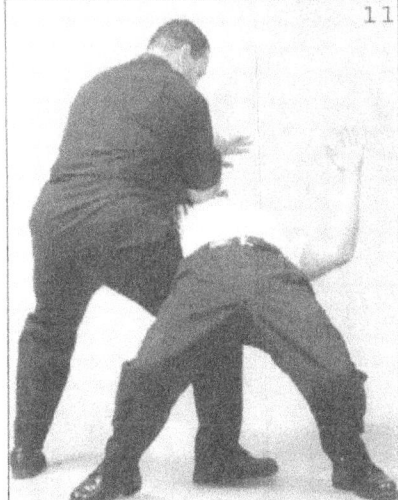

Start position (1). Strike to Ax 5 (2). Pull his arm toward you at a 45-degree angle (3). Turn your upper body toward him (4). Apply pressure to the elbow at the sternum (5). Apply a lock (6).

But what happens if he bends too far forward when you strike (7-8). Simply chin lift and apply a figure-four with a hip bump to imbalance (9). Now pull up on the lock and apply elbow pressure (10). Then pull up on the lock and balance the body over your leg to maintain control (11).

HAMMERLOCK

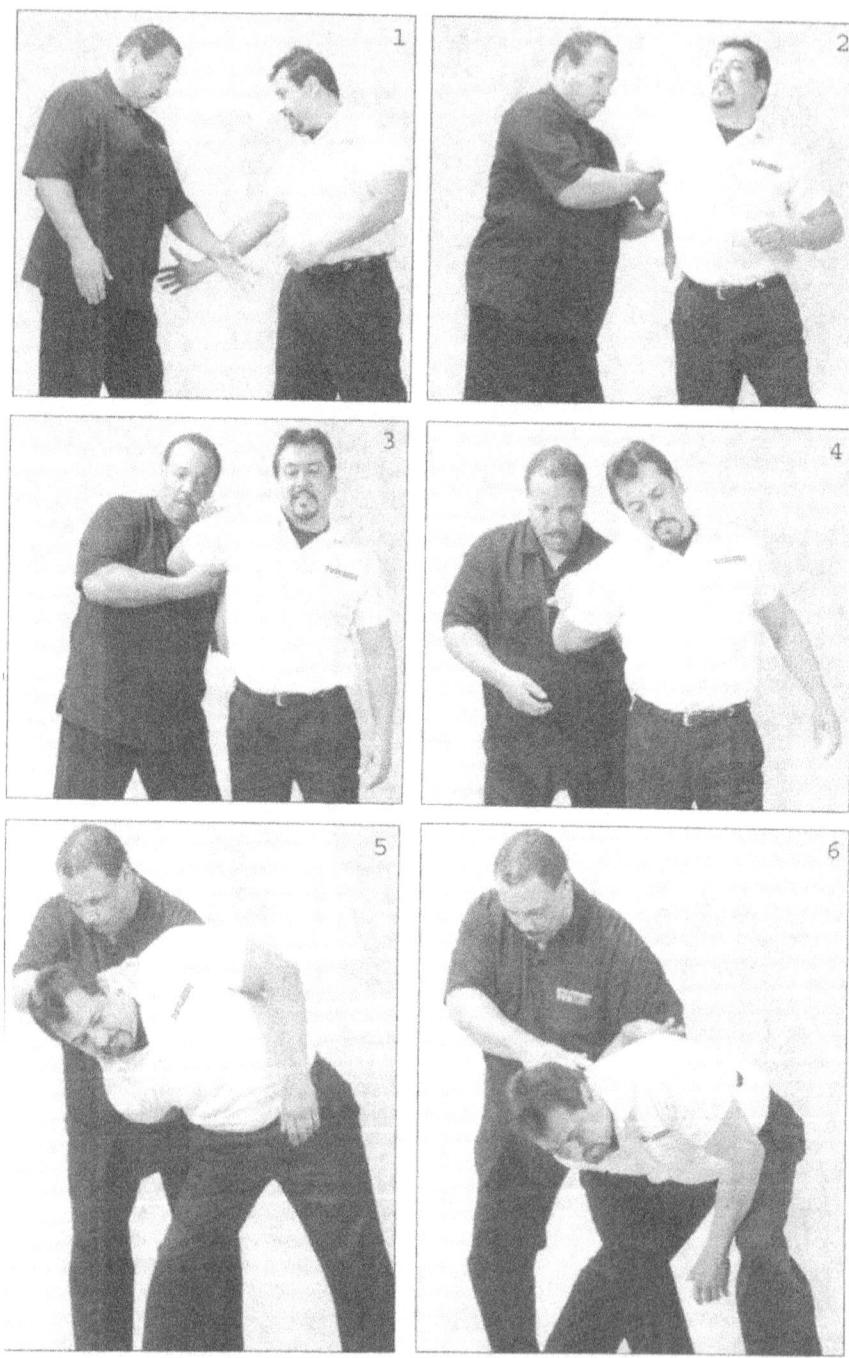

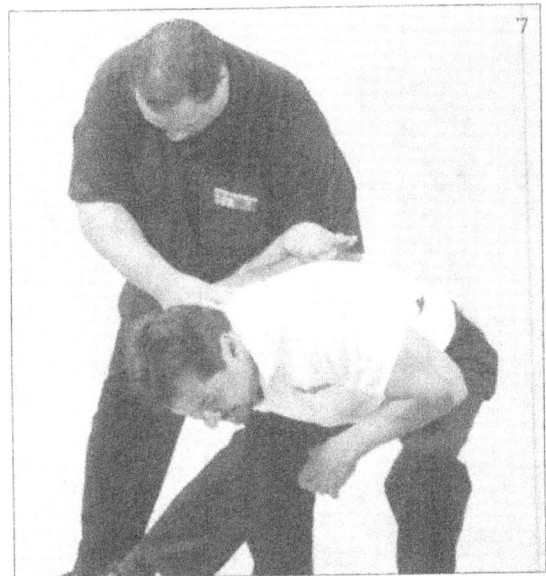

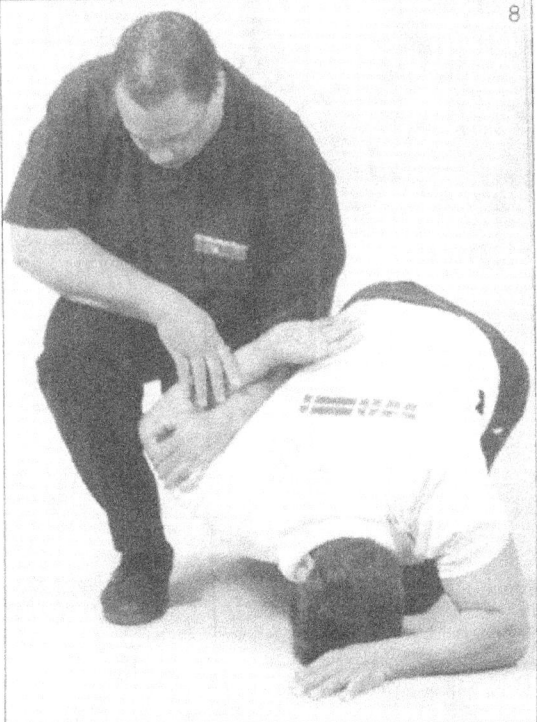

Start position (1). Put your right hand on the shoulder as the left hand snakes under the arm (2). Pressure is going up and forward (3). Apply pressure to your right to maintain control and balance (4). Apply pressure downward at a 45- degree angle (5). Bump his hip with your hip (6). This grounds him and puts him under control (7-8).

HAMMERLOCK

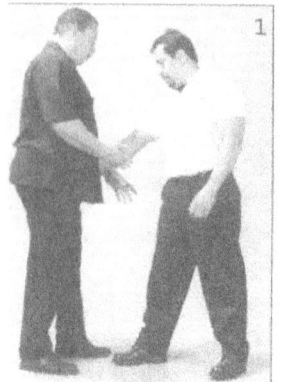

A grab is met with a reverse (1). I grab his elbow and pull him forward to break the plane (2). I chop to the rear of the neck (3). Keeping the lock tight to my body, I step sideways (4) and into a horse to drop him (5). Once on the ground I apply an arm bar (6). If needed, I can either knee or stomp him to the face (7).

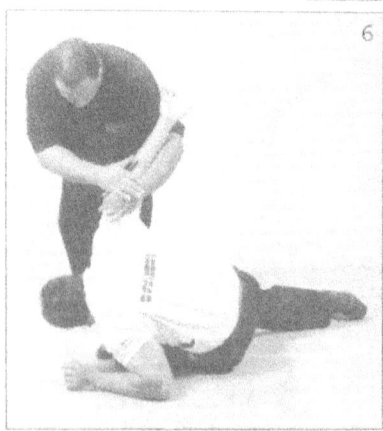
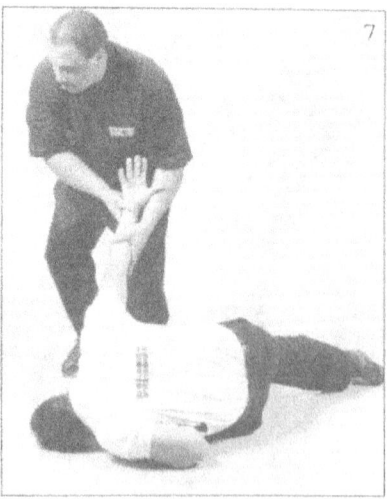

HAMMERLOCK

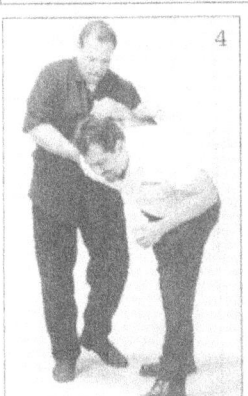
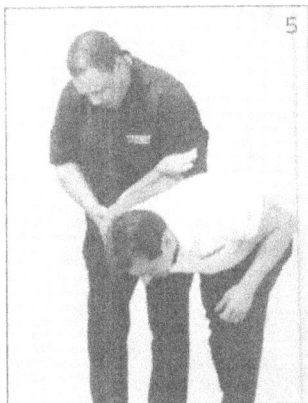

Grab the wrist (1) and punch to wood pile gall bladder liver (2). Lift his elbow and push in (3). Apply a lock (4). Now apply pressure downward and forward (5). Drop to your inside knee to ground opponent and control (6-7).

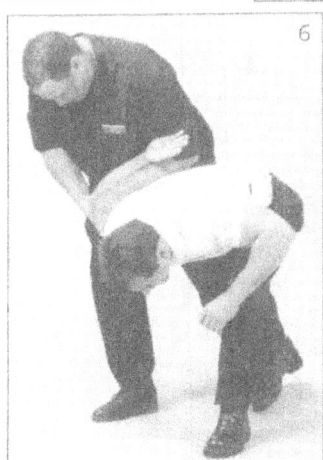
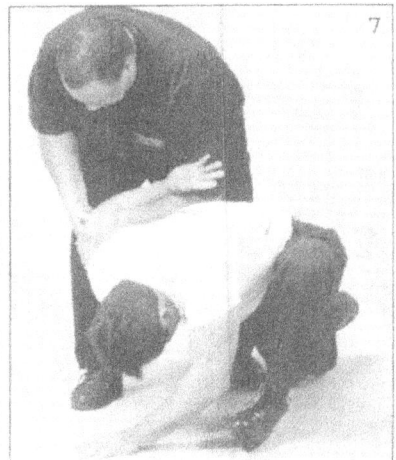

SHOULDER BRACE

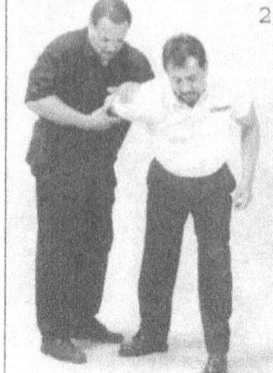

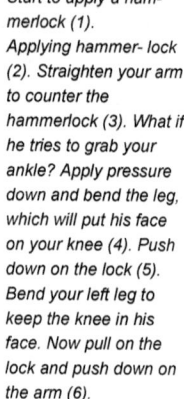

Start to apply a hammerlock (1).
Applying hammer- lock (2). Straighten your arm to counter the hammerlock (3). What if he tries to grab your ankle? Apply pressure down and bend the leg, which will put his face on your knee (4). Push down on the lock (5). Bend your left leg to keep the knee in his face. Now pull on the lock and push down on the arm (6).

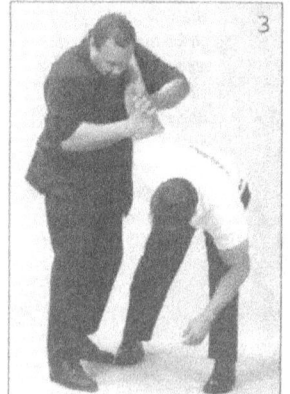

SHOULDER BRACE

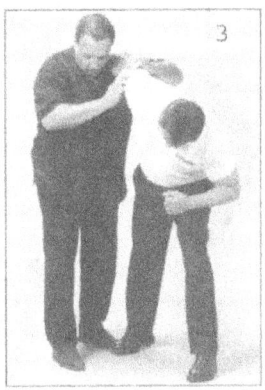

From the starting position (1), strike to wood pile (2). Apply a shoulder brace (3). Step across with a left leg to the outside of his left foot as you strike the back of the neck with your left hand (4). Turn clockwise and apply pressure on the neck and shoulder to throw (5). He will land face up in front of you (6). Control the arm as you turn and drop your right knee to his sternum (if required).

GOOSENECK

The assailant grabs my wrist (1). Push behind his elbow and countergrab his wrist (2). Knee to Wood 31 (3). As my left hand goes under his armpit, it helps straighten his arm (4). This places him into a gooseneck (5-6).

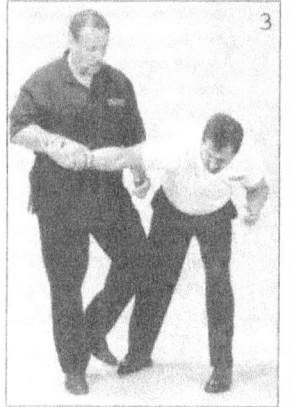

BODY BRACE

From a wrist grab (1), push his elbow away from you to take his balance (2). Step forward, grab his biceps and pull (3). Start to apply a gooseneck (4). Step behind and apply pressure down on the gooseneck (5). Push down and brace his body over your knee (6).

The Edge of WAR.

THE MARTIAL SCIENCE OF THE BLADE

The edge of W.A.R. addresses the use and defense of edged weapons. It begins with the proper grip and a mastery of the deadly D's — disruption, delay, deflection, disable, deadly force and inDexing. The four positions of edged weapons combat, ranges of combat and weapon retention are some of the basic concepts taught in this element of W.A.R.

The Martial Science of the Blade

This consists of:

a. The Grip of W.A.R. — **Alignment, aim and strength;**

b. The Deadly "D's" — **Disruption, Defense, Deflection, Disable, Deadly Force, and InDexing;**

c. **The Four Positions of Edged Weapons Combat;**

d. **Total Body Weapon Concept;**

e. **Tactical Positioning;**

f. **Forms of Attack;**

The Impact of W.A.R.

This teaches you how to use an impact weapon. We use the stick to strike, stroke, whip, smash or compress using either a one- or two-handed grip. Also taught are whole body usage and the stick for jointlocks, controls and takedowns.

THE USE OF IMPACT WEAPONS
a. Grip with one or both hands.
b. Whole weapon usage. Striking, stroking, circular, whipping, smashing, and compressing.
c. Whole body usage.
d. Immobilization: Jointlocks, controls and takedowns.

HOSTAGE RETRIEVAL
The skill to free a client, loved one or teammember from an attacker's grasp. This approach to unarmed combat teaches closed-door, open-door and back-door tactics. Included are the "bag pipe'" technique, proper use of force, and team tactics.

MULTIPLE AHACKERS
This is the element of the Within Arm's Reach program where all the preceding skills are tested and reinforced with principles to help you survive situations involving more than one attacker. You'll discover how to use awareness, proper mindset, eye-of-the-hurricane positioning, creating a delay, flow, and footwork. These are just a few of the concepts that form the W.A.R. framework.

CLOSE-QUARTER AGGRESSIVE FIREARMS
One of the highest levels of force options taught within the W.A.R. system.

The W.A.R. Chest

"Tools of the Trade"

The business of personal protection requires a number of dynamic and high-powered skills. They include: handgun training, protective and counterterrorism driving, paramedicine, and explosive recognition and search tactics. Also needed are personal combat skills involving impact and edged weapons.

But there also things we do everyday that surprisingly come into play more often than the "dynamic" variety. Some of the everyday tactics, equipment and techniques used in my Within Arm's Reach program are:

Tools of the Trade. What Cliff's "Go Bag" looks like from the outside.

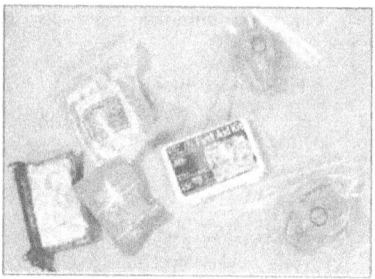

The "Go Bag" always includes plenty of medical provisions.

Whether he's ushering a client across town or jetting around the world, Cliff Stewart keeps a well-stocked back-up arsenal just in case.

Tools

1. **LEARNING TO SIT:** In a profession where moving quickly and dynamically can mean the difference between life and death, the simple act of sitting — or more importantly — sitting right, can make all the difference in the world.
   a. Center yourself in the middle of the chair.
   b. Keep your back straight and off the rear of the chair.
   c. Place your left leg forward and your foot flat on the ground at the outside front leg of the chair at 90 degrees.
   d. Your right leg is back halfway between the front and rear legs on the opposite side of your left leg. If this is your weapon side, the weight is on the ball of the foot.
   e. If your left side is your weapon side then place your right foot forward and your left foot halfway. The weight is on the ball of your foot.
   f. From this position you can immediately get up to stop an unwanted guest, become an obstruction between the threat and your client, use physical intervention

Cliff Stewart shows you the wrong way to sit and the wrong way to get up. His back is nestled against the chair (1). When he rises, his head is down (2) and his body is bent over and facing the floor (3).

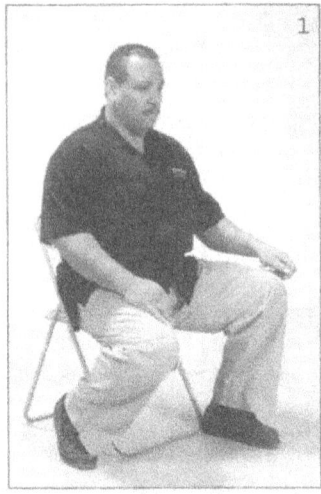
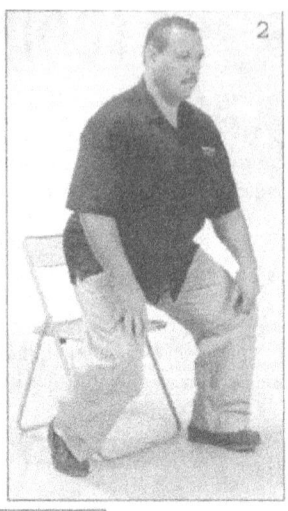

The right way to get up. His legs are spread and his right leg is bent at the knee (1). When he gets up from the chair, his head is up and his back straight (2). He stands straight, his hands are by his sides and he's prepared for anything (3).

2. SCANNING 360 DEGREES: Having eyes in the back of our head would be quite an advantage in this profession. But since we don't, let's see how we can make it seem like we're so blessed.

    a. Use peripheral vision to detect fuzzy objects and movement from the corner of your eyes.

    b. With deliberate eye movement to the left and right, you can extend your normal range of vision from 180 degrees to 200 degrees.

    c. You can also add to your field of vision by turning your head left and then right as far as you can. This can add up to 35 degrees to each side and improve your overall coverage to 270 degrees.

    d. While your feet are facing 12 o'clock, turn your torso 45 degrees in each direction. By adding deliberate rear eye movement and head turning you will have a full 360 degrees of observation. Practice using this technique while sitting or walking.

    e. A unique way to extend your vision to 360 degrees while minimizing head movement is to add to a hand mirror (the unbreakable type) to your 45-degree shoulder position. Extend the hand holding the mirror and tilt it up or down. Keep your shoulders stationary. This is perfect for fixed and semi-fixed assignments. I've used this technique primarily on television and movie sets for clients such as Mr. T and Joan Collins.

    f. THE DOOR SWING: Almost very picture depicts a bodyguard standing around a limo with at least one watching the client exit his vehicle. As Larry Flynt once told me, "Cliff, I'm not going to shoot myself. The problem will come from the other way." Get the message? You don't need to kiss up to the client to do your job. Attacks won't come from inside the car so scan the area around the vehicle.

Some bodyguards will look out while their client is getting out of the vehicle but be too far from the car to provide cover and make a quick escape. Always maintain your fields of responsibility (vision, fire and control) even as you are opening a door to a car or building. Here's how to do it:

    a. As your client approaches the car, your back should be facing the car at the right rear passenger side. You should be in a 360-degree scanning position.

    b. While still looking forward, open the door with your right hand.

    c. As your client gets within arm's reach let the hand behind your back grab the door.

    d. Open the door wide enough to allow you client to enter. Never stop your 360- degree scanning as he climbs into the car. Now step back and block the open area with your body, keeping the door at a angle to provide some protection.

    e. If the client wants to speak you can hear him while maintaining your area of responsibility.

    f. Once he's in the car you can close the door and assume the assigned position.

    g. If he needs to speak to you, kneel on one knee, keeping yourself as an obstruction between the street and your client. Pull the door closer to provide additional security, turn your head to listen but always be ready for any attack.

    h. By changing hands and stepping to the outside, you've given the client access to the inner car. Follow by stepping back when the client is inside and pulling the door first at an angle to close the space and help you provide an obstruction between the street and the inside of the car.

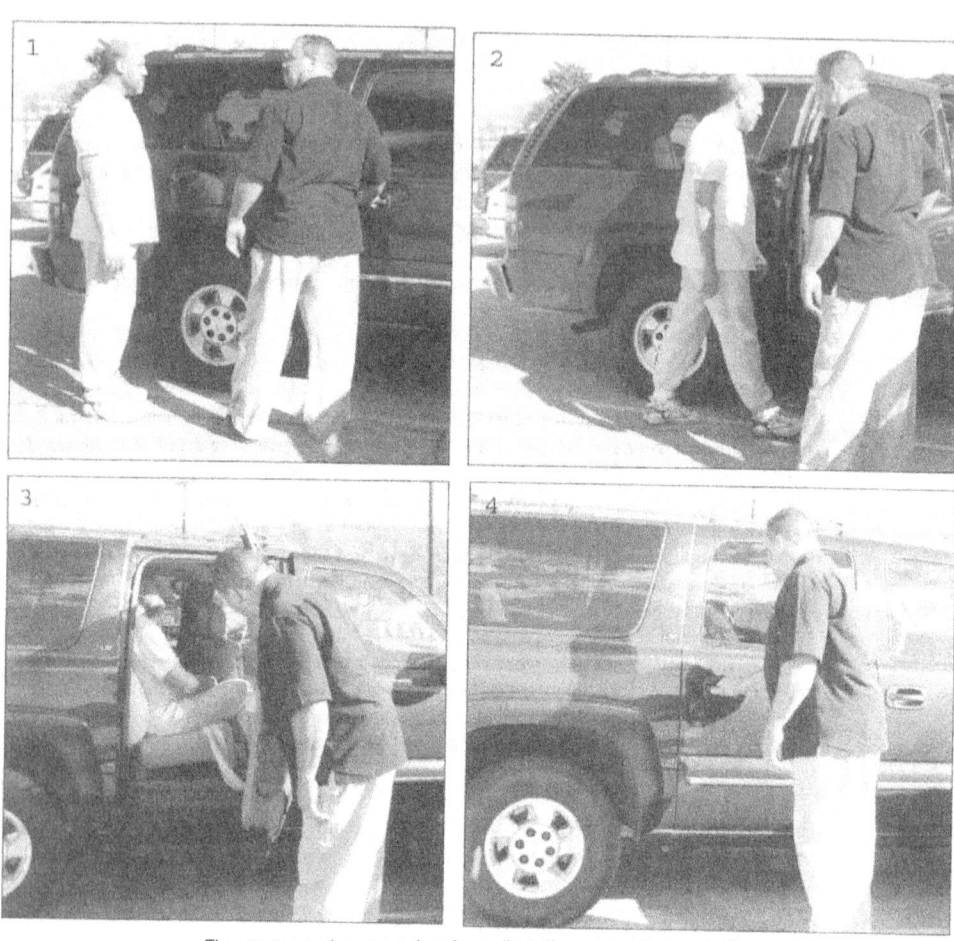

The wrong way to open a door for a client. If your back is turned (1), there's no way to scan for approaching attackers (2). Also, the client remains in full view of anyone with an agenda (3-4).

The right way to open a car door. With the client behind him, Cliff Stewart surveys his surroundings (1). Once he deems it safe, he opens the door with his left hand (2), while keeping the client out of striking or firing range (3). He then switches the door from his left to right hand (4) and closes it behind his client (5) without ever turning his back to the street.

4. **STOP THE RAIN AND UNWANTED PHOTOS:** Dealing with photographers has long been a major problem for stars and their protectors. Grabbing the camera and/or the photographer only gets the client and his protector in deeper trouble, because it can lead to criminal charges being filed against the protector and civil liability claims against the protector and client. Here's how to deal with the problem:

   a. First get the right equipment. Try to keep an oversized golf umbrella in the trunk next to your "Go Bag".

   b. If your client does not want to be photographed, carry the umbrella with you at all times. This tactic is used for outside movement. I first open the door to let the client out and then use the umbrella as a cove of protection. It also doubles as a pretty good crowd mover in a pinch. I position the umbrella so it can block the face of the client. I ask the client to lightly hold onto the inside umbrella frame, to keep his head up, and his nose pointing to the center and slightly up toward the inside top of the umbrella to maintain balance.

   I control the protective cove by holding the handle as close to the center as possible with my non-weapon hand; the other part is placed under my arm in the "bag pipe" position. My head remains above the umbrella while my weapon hand controls the outside rim in case I need to use the umbrella for defensive purposes.

   c. When I reach the car, I use the swing door technique. Make sure to use both the umbrella and your body as a shield for the client. I open the door with my weapon hand and back the client into the open door. The umbrella should also face the crowd and photographers.

   d. The key to making this technique work is the client must keep his head down while you open the door. At the same time, you must keep your head up and scan the area for potential trouble. As they reach the car, tell them to get in as quickly as possible.

   e. Now swing the umbrella away from the car until the inside of the umbrella and handle are facing the crowd and blocking its view. Keep your body in front of the door, pull up the umbrella until it just clears the car door, and slam the door shut.

   f.   Close the portable cove, throw it in the trunk or front seat and "get going".

5.   **"THE GO BAG":** Batman ain't got nothin' on us."

   In *Batman,* the movie, the Joker remarks, "Where does he get all those wonderful toys?" Batman is famous for carrying a utility belt that contains a wide variety of crime-fighting gadgets. Well, protection specialists also need an array of "wonderful toys" to prevent situations both unique and dangerous. And so we turn to a "Go- Bag," which is a utility belt for man-sized jobs. We sometimes need equipment we can't always carry on our person. Also, we often need to bring extra supplies in case the unexpected becomes reality.

   The size and type of equipment needed for your "Go-Bag" depends on the assignment, client and location. The basics of every "Go Bag" are the same. The "Bag" needs to be strong and lockable. You can use a briefcase, but carrying it occupies one of your hands. 1 prefer something with a shoulder strap so I have both hands free. It should contain:

   a. One trauma kit plus a trauma notebook.

   b. Sanitary napkins, Maxi pads and a small box of cellophane food wrap.

   c. Oversized cuffs and flex cuffs plus key and restraint cutters.

d. A micro-cassette recorder or digital recorder.
e. CPR microshield, bio-hand cleaner and thick latex gloves.
f. Pepper spray or Mace.
g. Portable alarms and door locks.
h. Two cameras — one for day use and other one equipped with a flash (the throwaway types are fine).
i. Batteries of all types, cell phone replacement batteries and a charger.
j. Flash lights.
k. Multi-purpose tool.
l. Night vision goggles and binoculars.
m. Back-up knife and watch.
n. A Zippo lighter, because its windproof, cold-proof and moisture-proof.
o. Space/survival blanket and a towel.
p. Warm-up suit or jump suit or jeans and a polo shirt, plus socks and an extra pair of shoes.
q. Small overnight kit.
r. Additional ammunition and magazines. Also bring your back-up gun, belt and holster.
s. Executive protection specialist handbook.
t. Map, compass or global locator.
u. Pens and note pads.

t entry permit on arrival

I

I r WMIGnrTION AUSTRALIA

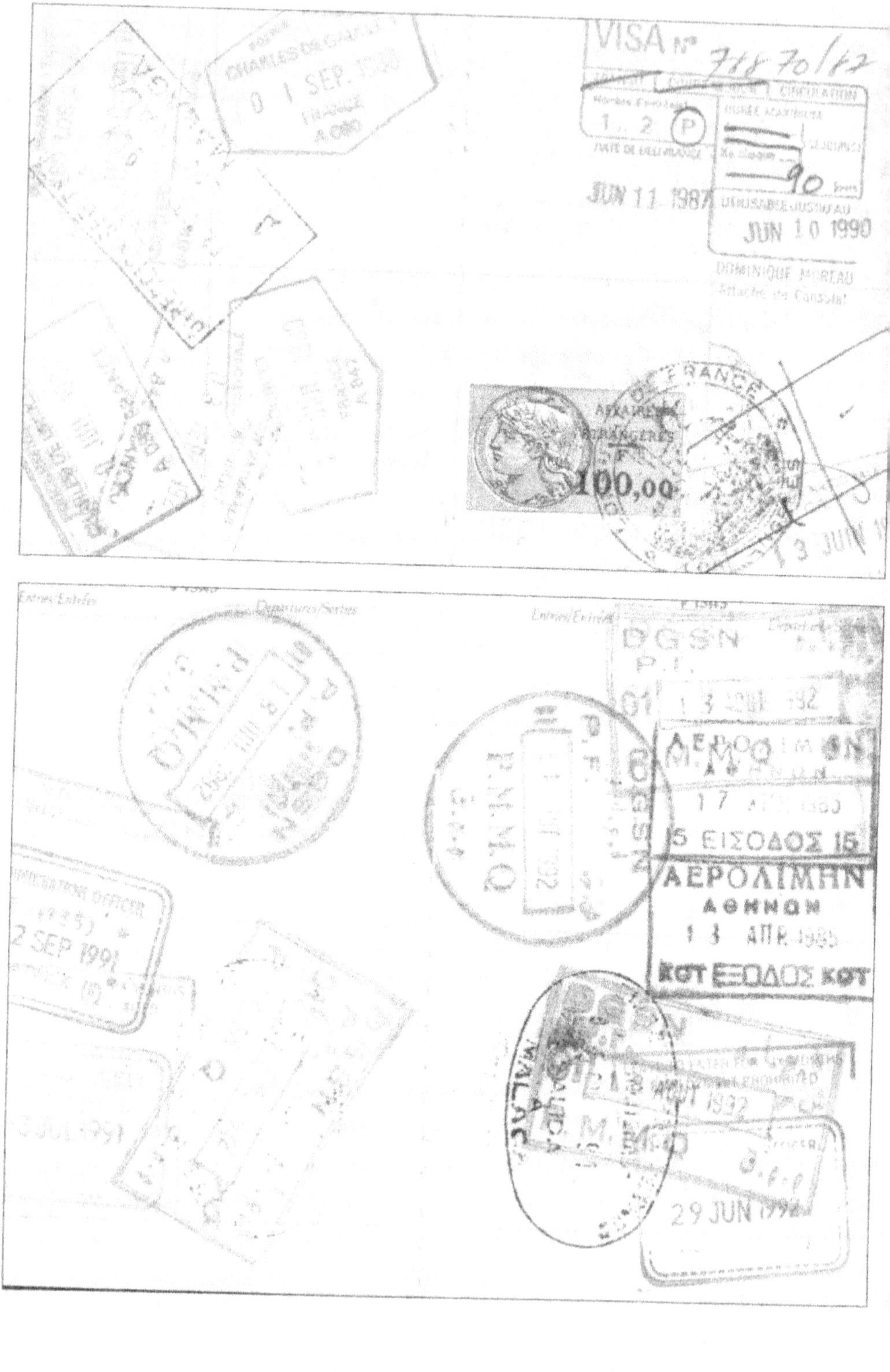
VISA N°
JUN 11 1987
JUN 10 1990
DOMINIQUE MOREAU
Attaché de Consulat
CHARLES DE GAULLE
FRANCE
AFFAIRES ETRANGERES
100,00
DGSN
ΕΙΣΟΔΟΣ
ΑΕΡΟΛΙΜΗΝ
ΑΘΗΝΩΝ
ΕΞΟΔΟΣ
2 SEP 1991
29 JUN 1992

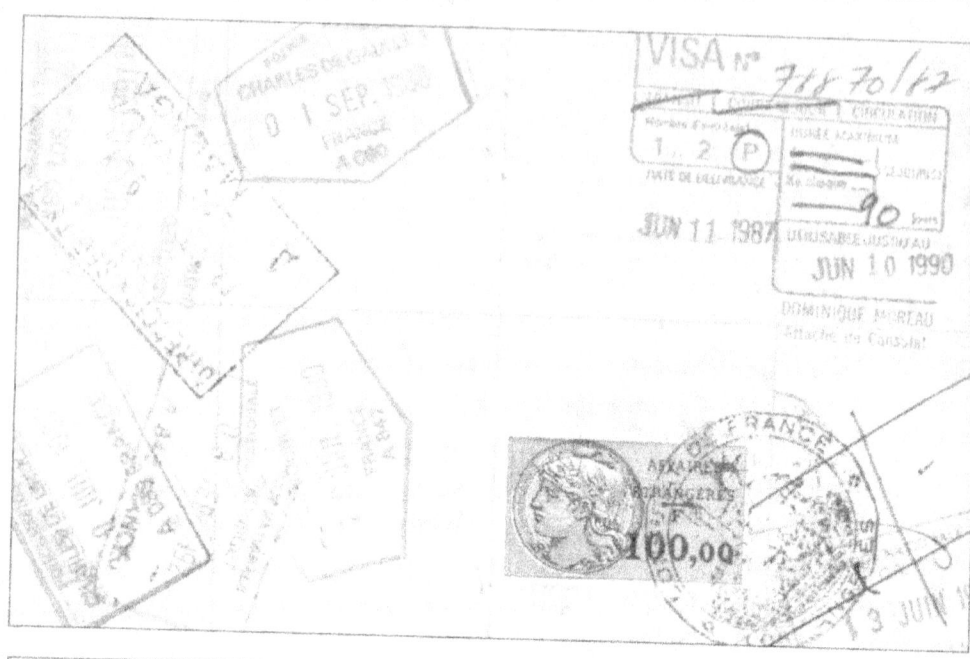

Definitions

Active Awareness: Monitoring for a specific purpose and specific clues.

Concentration: The focus of willpower and attention.

Courage: The ability to perform a task despite the danger and the possibility of physical, mental, social or psychological harm.

Desire: A passion to accomplish a particular mission, goal, and life statement or dream.

Ego Management: The skill of governing your courses of action that are influenced by poor self-esteem and personal uncertainty of what you think others think of you. **Fear:** The physical and psychological response to an incident — real or not — that triggers a number of physical, mental and psychological responses.

Fear Management: The skill of directing the fight-or-flight response used to enhance the ability to defend yourself and others.

Instinct Control: Managing distractions, which can be achieved by understanding the elements of protection, concentration and awareness.

Management: Governing actions that are influenced by emotional factors and elements.

Mindset: The mental and emotional acceptance of a particular course of action for an assault, attack or life-or-death fights.

W.A.R.riorship: The personal state of confidence developed and reinforced by proper training and a strong moral commitment to the value of all life. Also included is a personal and ethical code of conduct. The goal is to be the best you can be.

www.ingramcontent.com/pod-product-compliance
Lightning Source LLC
Chambersburg PA
CBHW070946230426
43666CB00011B/2576